DIVING
COZUMEL

DIVING
COZUMEL

BY STEVE ROSENBERG

AQUA QUEST PUBLICATIONS, INC. ▪ NEW YORK

PUBLISHER'S NOTE

The Aqua Quest *Diving* series offers extensive information on dive sites as well as topside activities.

At the time of publication, the information contained in this book was determined to be as accurate and up-to-date as possible. The reader should bear in mind, however, that dive site terrain and landmarks change due to weather or construction. In addition, new dive shops, restaurants, hotels and stores can open and existing ones close. Telephone numbers are subject to change as are government regulations.

The publisher welcomes the reader's comments and assistance to help ensure the accuracy of future editions of this book.

Good diving and enjoy your stay!

Library of Congress Cataloging-in-Publication Data

Rosenberg, Steve, 1948-
    Diving Cozumel / by Steve Rosenberg.
        p.   cm. — (Aqua Quest diving series)
    Includes index.
    ISBN 0-9623389-7-4 : $18.95
    1. Scuba diving—Mexico—Cozumel—Guidebooks.
    2. Cozumel (Mexico)—Guidebooks. I. Title. II. Series.
GV840.S78R644   1992
797.2'3—dc20   92-26488
                                        CIP

Cover: Large gray angelfish are common in Cozumel and are easy to photograph, especially on some of the shallower reefs like Paradise, where they are accustomed to being fed by divers.

All photographs are by the author unless otherwise noted.

Maps and line art by Justin Valdes.

Printed in Hong Kong
10 9 8 7 6 5 4 3 2 1

ACKNOWLEDGEMENTS

Thank you to all who contributed their time, effort and assistance in writing and illustrating this book.

I greatly appreciate the help and cooperation of Barbachano Tours, Darcy Communications, Mexicana Airlines and my old friends Tim and Patti Massimino at the Galapago Inn. Thank you also to Christie Rudd and Howie Perlin.

I would like to thank my dive buddies, Roger Hess, Greg Bassett and my wife Kathleen, who have been assistants, models, sherpas and friends throughout this project. In particular I would also like to thank Paul Padilla Perez, who always went out of his way to provide useful information, find unusual critters (including seahorses and batfish), lend a hand, and be a good friend.

A special thanks to Professor Bruce Heyer, a research biologist with the University of California for the information on Cozumel's oceanography.

Thank you to Jesse Cancelmo, Lisa Rooney-Zarri, Phil Zarri and Patrick Rooney for allowing me to use a few of their slides to fill in the gaps.

Finally, thank you to the many wonderful guides I have had the opportunity to dive with over the years.

CONTENTS

FOREWORD

Like countless other divers, my first warm water dive trip was to Cozumel. Since that trip some 14 years ago, I have returned to the island an average of once a year, either on photography assignments, or to lead dive groups and teach seminars.

A few things have changed over the years. Fast boats now make the southern sites more easily accessible and new construction has added to the luxury accommodations. But, there has been little change in the excellent quality of diving, and the warmth of the people and the atmosphere remain the same.

Cozumel has a year-round pleasant climate, warm clear water, friendly people, plenty of topside attractions, and some of the best diving in the entire Caribbean.

The island is especially known for its exceptionally clear, 150-foot visibility, and for its effortless drift diving. The lush reefs on the southwestern end of the island offer incredible drop-offs, pinnacles, and labyrinths of interconnecting caves and tunnels. In addition, the variety and abundance of marine life is exceptional. Photographers and video enthusiasts will find more friendly, 'easy to shoot' reef fishes, eels and invertebrates than on any other Caribbean island destination.

Thirty of Cozumel's most popular dive sites—both shore and boat dives—are covered in detail in this guide. For all of the primary sites a cross-section diagram is provided which shows the bottom profile and the depths of various points of interest. Also included is a chapter on Cozumel's interesting and unusual fishes and invertebrates.

There is also information on where to stay on Cozumel and suggestions on where to dine and shop. For those interested in exploring the island or the Yucatan Peninsula, there is a section devoted to the major points of interest, such as the extensive Mayan ruins and expansive beaches. Included are the small islands of Contoy and Mujeres.

From beauty and excitement underwater to plentiful topside activities, Cozumel offers something special for every member of the family.

Steve Rosenberg
Union City, California
October 1992

CHAPTER 1 ISLA DE COZUMEL

The Mexican island of Cozumel is located 12 miles (19 km) off the northeast coast of the Yucatan Peninsula. It is a small island—29 miles (47 km) long and 9 miles (15 km) wide—whose highest point is only 45 feet (14 m) above sea level. Cozumel is the largest of the three islands located off the northeast coast of Yucatan, the other two being Mujeres and Contoy to the north. Cancun, on the mainland, is about 30 miles (19 km) northwest of Cozumel. Cuba is about 95 miles (59 km) to the northeast.

The reefs of Cozumel are part of one of the largest barrier reefs in the world, the Belizean Reef, that extends south from the tip of Isla Mujeres 174 miles (280 km) to the Bay of Honduras.

THE PAST

The pre-Hispanic history of Cozumel is closely tied to the rise and decline of Mayan civilization. The Maya established themselves in Guatemala 15 centuries before the birth of Christ. Their culture and influence spread quickly throughout southern Mexico. By A.D. 200 they were building cities on the Yucatan Peninsula. The Mayan civilization was at its peak between the seventh and ninth centuries.

The Mayans, who originally inhabited the island, referred to it as *Ah-Cuzamil-Peten.* In their language this meant "Place of the Swallows," so named because of the great numbers of swallows and other birds that once nested there.

Beginning in the tenth century, the Mayan civilization began to decline. Their numbers were greatly eroded by famine, pestilence and incursions by the warlike Toltecs from western Mexico. By the twelfth century, the Toltec cult of *Quetzalcoatl,* meaning 'plumed serpent,' dominated the Mayan culture.

In 1518, the island was accidentally visited by Don Juan de Grijalva, who landed in Cozumel with four vessels bound for Cuba. The number of well constructed stone streets and buildings amazed him. At that time, the island was very prosperous and well populated. The following year Spaniard Hernan Cortes discovered the religious center and renamed it "Santa Cruz De Cozumel." He remained on the island long enough to desecrate the Mayan's temples. It is believed that Cortes was offended by the idolatrous rites and ceremonies he witnessed. Therefore, he ordered his men to tear down the idols and erect a statue of the Virgin Mary in their place. Consequently, few of these impressive structures exist on the island today.

Cortes used the island as a staging area for his initial assault on the Mexican mainland. After the influx of the Spaniards and the spread of smallpox, the population on Cozumel had dropped from the 40,000 reported by Cortes in 1519 to less than 300 by the year 1570.

In the late 1600's, the island became a refuge for many pirates, among them the well-known Jean Lafitte and Henry Morgan. These experienced sailors appreciated the safety and protection offered by the leeward side of the island against violent storms. The pirates obtained fresh water from the lagoon at Chancanab. They created general havoc with their drinking and fighting, disrupting the lives of the small population of Spaniards and Mayan Indians on the island. By 1843 the island of Cozumel was almost totally abandoned. In 1848, refugees from the turmoil on the mainland began to resettle the island.

Bright red torch ginger flowers grow readily in the tropical climate of Cozumel.

Cozumel again became a center of activity when the chewing gum industry began to flourish in the United States. For centuries, the Mayan people had been satisfying their thirst by chewing raw sap from the *zapote* tree that grows on Cozumel and throughout much of Central America. In the early 1900's, the developed world was introduced to this new sweet treat, bringing a short-lived economic boom to the mainland coast. The new shipping routes included Cozumel, which has one of the best harbors in the area suitable for large ships. A few companies made large fortunes from the nickel pack of chewing gum, while the Indians who hacked their way through the dense jungle to tap the trees struggled for a subsistence. Partly because of this search for chicle, magnificent ruins were uncovered deep in the forested jungles on the mainland, and to a lesser extent on the island of Cozumel itself.

The great pyramid of Uxmal, located south of Merida, is a good example of Mayan construction during the Classic Period. The ruins found throughout the Yucatan Peninsula are a silent reminder of the early history of Cozumel.

Synthetics, which are now used almost exclusively in the manufacture of chewing gum, eventually replaced the hard to get chicle.

During World War II, the United States built an airstrip on Cozumel and operated a submarine base. During this period, special diving teams came to the island to train before embarking to the European and Pacific theatres of war. These divers began to spread tales of the incredible visibility and majestic underwater reefs around the island.

After the war, the island returned to relative obscurity until 1961 when a television documentary produced by Jacques Cousteau introduced the wonders of the reef to the public. Cousteau declared that Palancar and the surrounding reefs were among the most beautiful in the world.

The Present

Since statehood in 1974, Quintana Roo, which includes Cozumel, has enjoyed a steady growth in tourism. By 1970, the population on the island had reached 10,000. Today there are almost 50,000 people living on Cozumel.

During the last few years, the number of

major resort hotels in Cozumel has greatly increased. However, it is unlikely that the island will ever grow into a high-rise city like Cancun because the island's water supply will not support an enormous increase of people. In addition, everything used or consumed on the island has to be shipped across the channel that separates Cozumel from the mainland.

Useful Information

Banks, Currency and Exchange Rates. Banks in San Miguel are open six days a week usually from 9:30 A.M. to 1:30 P.M. Most resorts can provide pesos in exchange for United States currency, and have posted rates and times that exchanges may be made. However, some resorts will not always be able to provide this service.

The exchange rate is adjusted daily. While exchange rates are usually best at banks, the rate at hotels is not usually much less. Mexican paper money comes in denominations of 500, 1,000, 2,000, 5,000, 10,000, 20,000 and 50,000 pesos. Coins come in denominations of 5, 10, 20, 200 and 500 pesos.

It is a good idea to exchange some American dollars for pesos at the airport. You will find that it is convenient to carry a small amount of pesos or at least US$20.00 in one dollar bills or the equivalent sum in pesos for taxis or tips. While almost everyone will accept United States dollars, United States coins are rarely accepted by any of the local merchants, including taxi drivers.

Climate. Because Cozumel lies only 9 miles (15 km) off the Yucatan coast, it reflects a more continental climate than the oceanic dominated islands of the eastern Caribbean. The warm, humid jungles of the mainland trap solar energy during the day and release it at night which keeps the evenings warm. As the night progresses and the land continues to cool, the surrounding warm sea buffers any extreme drop in air temperature. Thus, Cozumel enjoys warmer days than islands further offshore and warmer nights than on the mainland.

Average annual temperature is about 80°F (27°C). During the mid to late summer months temperatures can reach the low 90's F (about 33°C).

The rainy season begins in June and often lasts through October. During this period, it may rain daily and humidity is higher than during other periods. However, the frequent afternoon showers are usually brief. From November through May it is generally balmy with lower humidity and an occasional cool evening.

In the winter months from December through February, cold fronts sweeping across the North American continent from the northeast can cause occasional overcast conditions and drop air temperatures to 72°F (22°C).

Dining and Night Life. The warm, balmy evenings of Cozumel offer a variety of exciting nighttime activities. Every visitor should sample the food at some of the excellent restaurants, stroll among the lights and sounds of San Miguel, and pop into one of the outrageous discos.

Electricity. The electricity at most resort hotels is reputedly 110 volt/60 cycle, the same as in the United States. However, more often than not the output ranges between 128 and 134 volts during the day, and 116 to 130 volts at night. This can cause serious damage to some electronic equipment, such as rechargeable strobes and chargers. If you have a voltage meter, test the output of the electrical sockets. If the current is over 120 and your charger is only meant to accept 110 volts, charge your batteries or battery packs for several short intervals, rather than for the recommended charge time. In any event, monitor the charger to see how fast it heats up. Don't let it get hot to the touch, or you may damage the electronic components.

Entry and Exit Requirements. A passport or proof of citizenship (for United States citizens a certified copy of a birth certificate, voter's registration card, or notarized affidavit) is needed to obtain a tourist card to get into Cozumel. In an emergency, airline personnel can assist you in obtaining an emergency notarized affidavit as proof of citizenship. You will be issued a temporary Mexican Tourist Card upon departing the United States, or on the plane flying into Mexico. The tourist card will then be stamped when you go through immigration at the airport after you land. Retain this document because it must be presented upon departure, along with payment of a departure tax of approximately US$15.00. If you enter Cozumel by international carrier, you must go through immigration, pick up your luggage and then clear customs.

The airport on Cozumel is about 1.9 miles (3 km) from downtown San Miguel. Whether you come to Cozumel by international carrier or domestic airline, stop off at the transportation desk to purchase a ticket to your hotel or resort. The rates are posted on the wall behind the counter for hotels in given areas. The fare is approximately US$1.00 for hotels in San Miguel, and US$3.00 to US$4.00 per person for hotels and resorts outside town.

You will receive a receipt from the clerk, which you should then give to your taxi or mini-bus driver as soon as your bags are stowed in the vehicle. Make sure that all your bags are loaded before you leave the airport and make sure they all get off with you at your destination. On Cozumel luggage porters are eager to help you transfer your bags to the waiting taxis and US$.50 per heavy bag is a reasonable fee.

In addition to traveling by air, there are frequent ferry trips between Cozumel and the Yucatan mainland. Also, large cruise ships routinely visit the island, off loading swarms of eager shoppers and snorkelers.

Getting There. There are a number of international air carriers serving the island, including Mexicana and Continental. Domestic flights also arrive daily from the Mexican mainland. AeroCozumel schedules connecting flights from Cancun International Airport several times a day.

Island Driving. Driving around the main part of the island is easy. The island is flat and the roads are well cared for. There is a single main road that circles the southern two thirds of the island. San Miguel, which has a laid back, unhurried atmosphere, is the only town on the island of Cozumel. Here there is a wide selection of restaurants and an endless number of souvenir, clothing, jewelry and department stores. The Plaza del Sol, located in the center of town along the shore road, has a number of modern civic buildings. The Plaza affords a meeting place where townspeople gather for festivals, celebrations or friendly chats. The streets that immediately surround the plaza are closed to vehicular traffic, making it a pleasant area to stroll and watch the goings-on.

In San Miguel the roads are laid out in a grid pattern. The roads running north and south have the right of way, and you must yield or

stop at all intersections when driving on roads running east and west. There are also many one-way roads. The shore road in San Miguel is named Avenida Rafael Melgar. This main road is also referred to as the *Malecon* or seawall. The main roads running parallel to Avenida Rafael Melgar in a north/south direction (parallel to the coast), are *avenidas* (avenues) numbered in increments of five. Avenida Benito Juarez is the main road running east to west. This road becomes the Cross Island Highway at Avenida 65. All numbered avenues on the south side of Avenida Benito Juarez are designated *Sur* (south) while those on the north are designated *Norte* (north).

The main roads running east to west in San Miguel are designated as *Calles* (streets). *Calles* are even numbered on the north side of Avenida Benito Juarez and odd numbered on the south side of Avenida Benito Juarez.

Avenida Benito Juarez begins adjacent to the Plaza in San Miguel by the passenger ferry dock and cuts straight across the middle of the island.

If your vehicle breaks down, you may be assisted by the Mexican Tourist Department sponsored "Green Angels," who patrol the main roads during daytime hours.

The state owned Premex gas station, located in San Miguel on the southwest corner of the intersection of Benito Juarez Avenue and 30th Avenue, is the only gas station on the island. Gas is available in two grades, *Nova* (regular) in the blue pump and *Extra* (unleaded) in the silver pump.

Driving in Cozumel is on the right side of the road, passing is on the left. All the speed limits, distance markers and speedometers are in kilometers. A kilometer equals 5/8 of a mile or conversely, a mile is equivalent to about 1.6 kilometers.

Rental Vehicles. If you want a little more freedom, or if you want to explore the outlying areas of the island, you may want to rent a vehicle. Before renting a vehicle you must be able to show the rental agency your driver's license, a passport and a major credit card. Rates are approximately US$55.00 to US$60.00 per day. Collision insurance, which only covers 80 percent of any damages incurred, is well worth the approximately US$8.00 per day extra. Relatively speaking, it isn't that much money, and it may save you an

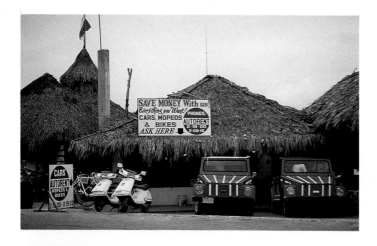

The paved roads on Cozumel are all flat and easily explored by moped or car. Rentals can be arranged through your hotel or resort.

Street merchants are found throughout downtown San Miguel, selling fresh fruit, fast foods and souvenirs.

incredible number of hassles. Be aware that in Mexico, your American car insurance is not valid.

When renting a vehicle, try to get one early in the day. There is a big difference in the quality of cars or mopeds that are available. Always inspect the vehicle thoroughly before you take it and have the agent write down any dents, scratches, missing equipment, and broken or non-operating windows. Check to see that the car is running properly, including forward and reverse gears, lights, brakes and horn. Also, make sure that the tires are not bald, and insure that there is a good spare tire and a jack.

Jeeps and Volkswagens are the most common passenger rental cars on the island. However, most of the rental cars are two-wheel drive, so you should not travel over rugged terrain, especially the very bad roads at the north end of the island.

Shopping San Miguel. There are many things to do in San Miguel. Most visitors take a break

from diving and relaxing to spend at least a couple of hours shopping. Cozumel is a duty-free port, and therefore offers many bargains. Of course, the best bargains you will find are on native merchandise, such as arts and crafts for which Mexico is famous. Among the most sought after items are clothing, jewelry, Mexican liquor and souvenirs. Bargaining with vendors is no longer a wide spread practice on the island, and established stores will not dicker at all on their marked prices unless business is slow or they are advertising a sale.

Black coral and silver are available in a wide assortment of unique jewelry designs and at very reasonable prices. One of the best places to pick up a unique pair of earrings or an unusual pendant made of black coral is at **Roberto's**. This shop, which is owned and operated by Cozumel's foremost black coral artisan, is located in the Barracuda Hotel at No. 618 Rafael Melgar a few blocks south of the Plaza.

Most of the shops and boutiques offer the

Beautiful sunsets are a common attraction on Cozumel's west coast. Many visitors to the island enjoy a relaxing evening, strolling along the beaches or swinging leisurely on seaside hammocks.

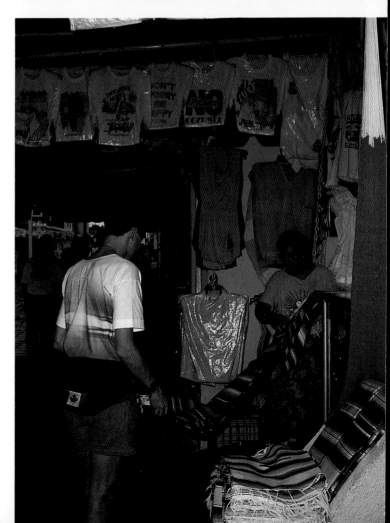

Among the most popular items tourists shop for are locally made clothing and blankets.

standard variety of souvenirs. A few of these shops have unique or sizable collections. **Alegria Infantil**, located on 5 Avenida Norte has some interesting and unusual children's toys. **La Concha**, located on 5 Avenida Sur, about a half block from the Plaza, is one of the better quality gift shops, displaying folk art from all over Central America including colorful Guatemalan weaving. There is no end of jewelry stores with high quality silver earrings, necklaces and pendants, including **Van Cleef's** in the Plaza del Sol Mall and **Tiffany's** at Calle 2 Norte #9.

Siestas and Business Hours. Cozumel still observes the traditional Mexican custom of the afternoon siesta during the heat of the day. For most shops, business hours Monday through Saturday are usually 8:00 or 9:00 A.M. to 1:00 or 2:00 P.M., reopening at 4:00 or 5:00 P.M. until 8:00 or 9:00 P.M. Of course, when cruise ships are in port, many shops stay open throughout the day to take advantage of the surge in business patrons. Also, siesta hours don't apply to most eating establishments, which open early and stay open until 10:00 or 11:00 at night.

Taxis. Getting around Cozumel is fairly easy for visiting divers. Most visitors rely exclusively on taxis or simply walk between destinations. Taxis are closely controlled in Cozumel, so that the rates between given destinations are the same.

Always ask the driver for the quantity (*quanto*) of money the ride will cost before you get into the taxi. Technically, the drivers should strictly adhere to standard rates, but there are often special circumstances when you may get charged a little more than usual. By law, standard taxis can carry a maximum of five passengers.

Getting a taxi is no problem in most parts of Cozumel. If you are in a heavily trafficked area, all you have to do is stand on the sidewalk and wave at the first empty taxi that goes by. In town, taxis line up along the shore road in the middle of town and take passengers in order. Also, any hotel will be happy to call a taxi for you.

Time Zone. Cozumel is in the Central Time Zone and does not observe Daylight Savings Time.

Water. *Turista*, also known as Montezuma's Revenge, is a common worry among visitors to Cozumel as well as the other areas of Mexico.

This illness is certainly no fun. It can cause uncomfortable cramping, chills, nausea, diarrhea, fever, dehydration and an overall fluish feeling. It is believed to be caused by, among other things, a strain of bacteria that often shows up in water or on uncooked food that is washed in unpurified water. Because the bacteria must get inside you to do the damage, consuming water or drinks that have ice cubes or eating fruits and vegetables washed in unpurified water are common ways to ingest the bacteria.

With a few precautions and by using a sensible approach to what you eat and drink, you can be fairly certain that you will avoid this unpleasant condition. The water is safer on Cozumel than in various other parts of Mexico because most of the water is well water. Also, most of the big hotels and resorts are now serving purified drinking water and ice made from purified water. In some of the larger resort hotels, such as **Club Cozumel Caribe** and the **Fiesta Americana Sol Caribe**, even the tap water is drinkable because they have their own desalinization systems.

However, to be safe, keep the following in mind:

- Get bottles of purified water to keep in your room for drinking and brushing your teeth. Drink one or two quarts of purified water every day to prevent dehydration.
- When you have water with your meals, ask whether the water is purified. When you have drinks with ice, make sure that the ice was made with purified water.
- Use common sense when you go out to eat. If you eat vegetables or salads, they are not always washed in purified water. Fruit with a thick skin that must be peeled is safe. Cooked foods are usually safe because the cooking kills the bacteria.

One should also keep in mind that a drastic change in diet often causes some of the same symptoms. What is often thought to be *Turista* is just your body's way of saying "enough" to a sudden onslaught of too much fresh fruit, spicy food or other things that you don't usually eat or drink.

CHAPTER **II** ACCOMMODATIONS

The newer and more modern hotels and resorts are located on the shore or across the street from the water, and are either north or south of the town of San Miguel. Most of these hotels offer on-site bars, restaurants, pools, air-conditioning, palm-shaded beach areas, and either on-site dive shops or diving activities provided by one of the excellent independent dive operators.

Hotels in the town of San Miguel are generally less expensive as they are located away from the shore. They are, however, within easy walking distance of cafes, restaurants, shops and the main Plaza. There is a fairly wide diversity of rooms available. Some of these are small and sparsely furnished, while some are luxurious, and offer such additional amenities as central courtyards, restaurants, bars and comfortable gathering places or meeting rooms. Most have private baths. Some hotels and condominiums also offer rooms with kitchens. These facilities can be a great bargain for families or close-knit groups. Almost all hotels have ceiling fans and/ or air-conditioning.

Normally, rates for all hotels and resorts are higher from the middle of December through Easter week. A 10 to 15 percent room tax is added to all quoted rates for hotels.

A note on hotel beaches. Most hotels on Cozumel have access to a beach for swimming and sunning, which is indicated in the hotel box which follows. Some of these beaches are large and sandy, and slope down into the water. Others may simply be a stretch of sand above the ironshore bank with steps going into the water. In addition, while most hotels are close to the water some are across the street from the water. In this case you may have to cross the road (usually via a tunnel or bridge) to access the beach. If a large, sandy beach is important to you, be sure to ask your travel agent or dive center what type of a beach a resort has. Remember that all of the beaches on Cozumel are open to the public.

To telephone Cozumel from the United States add **011-52-987** before the five-digit local number.

There is an extensive reef structure at Punta Sur with caves, caverns and tunnels extending well below 130 feet (39 m). Here a diver examines a large brown tub sponge.

	Rooms/Units	Air Conditioning	Tennis	Beach	Pool	Restaurant	Bar	Dive Operation	Gear Storage
North of San Miguel									
Cabanas Del Caribe Tel: 20017	48	■		■	■	■	■		
Hotel Cantarell Tel: 20144	98	■		■	■	■	■		
Club Cozumel Caribe Tel: 20100	260	■	■	■	■	■	■	■	■
Coral Princess Club Tel: 22822/22911	48	■		■	■	■	■		
El Cozumeleno Tel: 20344/20050	100	■	■	■	■	■	■		
Mara Tel: 20300/20149	50	■		■	■	■	■		
Melia Mayan Plaza Tel: 20411	188	■	■	■	■	■	■	■	■
Playa Azul Tel: 20199	60	■	■	■	■	■	■		
Downtown									
Bahia Tel: 20209	27	■							
Meson San Miguel Tel: 20233	97	■			■	■	■		
Safari Inn Tel: 20101	41	■							
Vista Del Mar Tel: 20545	33	■			■	■			
Vista Del Rey Tel: 21600	43	■			■	■	■		

	Rooms/Units	Air Conditioning	Tennis	Beach	Pool	Restaurant	Bar	Dive Operation	Gear Storage
South of San Miguel									
Barracuda Tel: 20002	51	■		■		■	■	■	
Casa Del Mar Tel: 21900/21665	129	■		■	■	■	■	■	■
El Presidente (Stouffer) Tel: 20923	259	■	■	■	■	■	■	■	
Fiesta Inn Tel: 22811	180	■		■	■	■	■		
Galapago Inn Tel: 20663	89	■		■	■		■	■	■
Holiday Inn (Cozumel Reef) Tel: 22622	207	■	■	■	■	■	■		
La Ceiba Tel: 20844	284	■	■	■	■	■	■	■	■
La Perla Tel: 20188	22	■		■	■	■	■	■	
Plaza Las Glorias Tel: 22000	163	■		■	■	■	■	■	
Scuba Inn Tel: 20145	192	■		■		■	■	■	
Sol Caribe (Fiesta Americana) Tel: 20700	322	■	■	■	■	■	■	■	
Villablanca Tel: 20730	50	■	■	■	■		■		

CHAPTER III   DINING

Cozumel has a wide assortment of places to eat ranging from elegant restaurants to fast food stands. You don't need directions to most restaurants; just give the name to the taxi driver. It is advisable to obtain reservations for dinner at the restaurants located in town, especially during peak season from mid-December through Easter. Reservations may be arranged by your hotel staff.

Many of the hotels and resorts have their own restaurants, some of which are excellent. At several hotels a package price is available that includes lodging, diving and meals. For example, the diving packages at the **Galapago Inn** and the **Club Cozumel Caribe** include meals. The restaurant at the Galapago Inn has a wide variety of delicious and authentic Mexican dishes, as well as a few American offerings. The Club Cozumel Caribe offers an extensive buffet, that varies nightly.

Most resorts and hotels, however, don't include all meals in their packages even though they have excellent restaurants. The **La Ceiba's** restaurant is now among the better restaurants on the island. At the end of 1990, the hotel brought in a well-known New York chef to revamp the restaurant from top to bottom. Listed below is a sampling of recommended restaurants.

Carlos N' Charlies is a famous "upstairs" bar and restaurant located on the waterfront. If you want to go where the action is, come on up.

San Francisco Beach has a couple of restaurants and, of course, Pancho's Bar where you can get an inviting tropical libation after a day of diving.

Aquario Restaurant   21097

The Aquario is located just south of San Miguel, less than a half mile from the Plaza el Centro on the shore road, Avenida Rafael Melgar S. The decor of this fancy restaurant mirrors the specialties of the house which are fish and lobster dishes. Inside there are huge aquariums filled with a variety of Cozumel's brightly colored reef fishes. Outside and behind the restaurant, there are open cement ponds full of interesting marine life including turtles, large green moray eels and nurse sharks.

Donatello's Restaurant   22586

Donatello's is located at 131 Melgar Ave Sur about a half-block from the downtown park facing the ocean. This is an elegant Italian restaurant which features scampi, lobster, veal and delicious pasta dishes.

El Paisa

El Paisa is located at 601 Hidalgo, near the intersection of Hidalgo and Calle Felipe Angeles. Try their delicious chicken cooked Mayan style or garlic conch, and perhaps one of their delightful cantaloupe spritzers with a light egg flan for dessert.

El Morro   23029

El Morro is just off Avenido Benito Juarez at 85 Norte Sur. Try their *camerones* (shrimp) with garlic or one of their excellent grouper dishes. El Morro also has a dance floor to work off a few of the calories. Don't forget to ask the cooks for a dance.

Ernesto's Fajitas Factory   20145

Ernesto's Fajitas Factory, located on hotel row between the Sol Caribe Hotel and Casa Del Mar, specializes in an assortment of tasty fajitas, including shrimp, chicken, and beef. The cooks prepare the fajitas with an entertaining flourish. This is a great place to go for a light dinner or a festive lunch after a morning of diving.

Morgan's   20584

This elegant and romantic dinner spot is in the main part of San Miguel on the north side of the Plaza. The specialties here are continental and Mexican dishes. The waiters make a flaming crepes suzette dessert which, when coupled with a variety of nightly musical entertainment, is one of the best after-dinner shows in town. It is open daily from 11 A.M. to 11 P.M.

Pancho's Backyard   22141

Pancho's is located inside the Los Cinco Soles store at 8th Street, on the waterfront north of the main plaza. Its excellent Mexican cuisine is served on a patio lined with water fountains.

Pizza Rolandi   20946

Pizza Rolandi, located four blocks north of the Plaza on Avenida Rafael Melgar, is an absolute must. Sit in the enclosed outdoor courtyard, and enjoy one of their excellent pizzas, the *Rolandi* (calzone), or their delicious lasagne. Begin the meal with their unusual garlic bread, a puff flour tortilla made from pizza dough and covered with loads of garlic, and finish off the meal with a pitcher of very special sangria.

Sports Page   21199

The Sports Page is on the north side of the Plaza on the corner of Calle Norte 2 and 5 Avenue Norte. This American-style restaurant and "video" bar features steaks, hamburgers, lobsters and chicken. The establishment's satellite dish antenna can pick up stateside sports networks, including important playoffs and championship games.

Chancanab Reef has an unusually large number of huge spiny lobsters prowling the interior caves and tunnels of the reef.

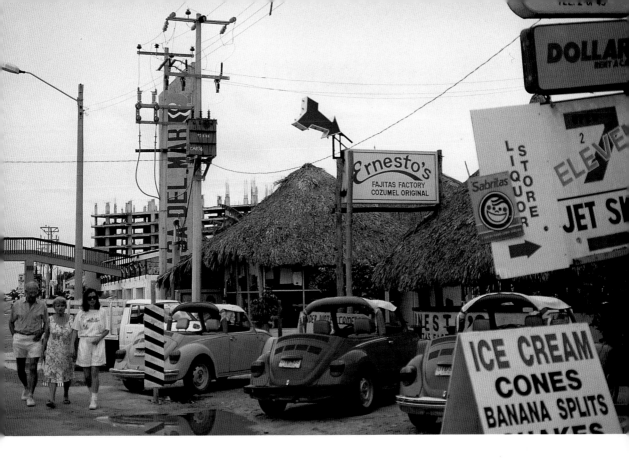

Ernesto's Fajitas Factory on hotel row is a very popular place to stop off for lunch or dinner.

CHAPTER IV SIGHTSEEING

COZUMEL

Archaeological Sites

Scattered around the island are many sites of Mayan ruins, some of which are difficult to reach. Most of these ruins are of the oratorio type that are characterized by small, square buildings built low to the ground with short entry ways and interior doors.

The well-preserved **San Gervasio** Mayan ruins cover an area of approximately 10 acres (4 ha), and have recently been excavated and restored. This site, the largest on the island, is located at the end of a new toll road approximately 6 miles (10 km) north of Avenida Juarez, east of San Miguel in the middle of the island. Guides, fluent in English, give groups of tourists detailed historical information on the site as you stroll beneath the tall trees. An afternoon visit to these ruins is time well spent.

Another site is **El Cedral**, located at the end of a 2-mile (3.2 km) dirt road which leaves the shore road just south of San Francisco Beach. El Cedral, while often visited, is small and not very impressive, but it is the oldest Mayan structure on the island. A few traces of paint and stucco of the original Mayan artist remain. It is believed that this ruin was once a major site. In the 1800's it was used as a local jail. A tree grows from its roof with thick exposed roots tangled in and around the stones of the ancient structure.

Another small site is **Tumba del Caracol** located on the east side of the dirt road to the Point Celarain Lighthouse near the south end of the island. This is a good place to stop for a snapshot.

Beaches

Cozumel has some outstanding beaches for sunning, swimming, snorkeling and other water sports. Along the main road on the west shore, there are a number of beach "clubs" which are bars and water sportcenters for tourists. **Chancanab Lagoon** and **San Francisco Beach** are the two most popular sites on the western shore.

Chancanab is a National Park located 5$^{1/2}$ miles (9 km) south of San Miguel. The Park has a large sandy beach, a botanical garden containing over 400 species of tropical plants, a huge natural seawater aquarium and a restaurant. Part of the Park is an underwater preserve for snorkelers and divers.

San Francisco Beach is a 2-mile (3.2 km) long sand beach which is mostly a hot spot for the non-diving set. There is a restaurant, live music, para-sailing and an assortment of other water related sports. Some dive operations still visit San Francisco Beach or one of the nearby beaches to have lunch between dives on two-tank trips.

Tulum is the site of a carved descending god, sometimes referred to as the "diving god." Photo: Phil Zarri.

MUSEUM OF THE ISLAND OF COZUMEL

For a good understanding of Cozumel's natural environment and exciting history, be sure to schedule a visit to the Museum. The four permanent exhibit halls provide information of particular interest to divers. These include a relief map of Cozumel, showing the relative ocean depths around the island, and 3-dimensional displays of the reefs depicting varieties of fishes, corals and reef structures. There are also charts and models that reveal how the reefs were formed. Perhaps the most important reason for divers to visit the Museum is that it graphically points out the potential harm from careless divers.

The Museum is located on Avenue Rafael Melgar, $2^{1/2}$ blocks north of the Plaza between 4th and 6th streets. The telephone number is 21007.

A tourist poses with a trio of trained iguanas at San Francisco Beach.

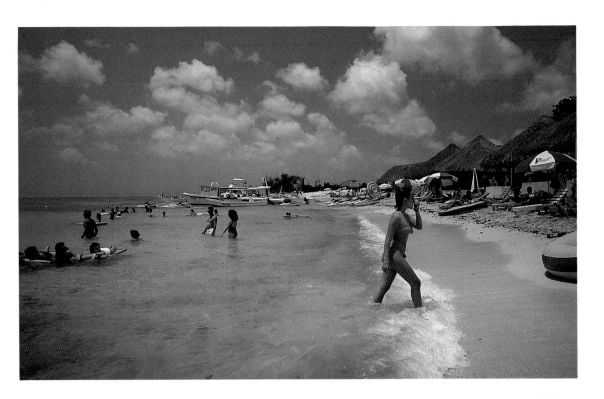

San Francisco Beach offers a wide variety of water sports, including swimming, snorkeling, parasailing and jet-skiing.

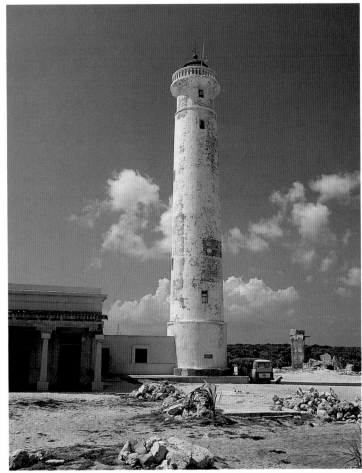

The tall, white lighthouse at Punta Celarain is worth a visit. Ask permission to climb to the top for a beautiful 360 degree view of the surrounding area.

The east side of the island gets a lot of heavy breaking surf on long, empty beaches. Although the surf is beautiful to observe and the warm water invites a swim, there are dangerous undercurrents along much of the shore. However, there are several safe places to swim and snorkel. There is a good protected beach where the cross island road reaches **Playa Oriente**. Here you will also find a popular bar named **Mescalito's**.

Farther south along the east shore, there are three safe and excellent beaches: **Punta Morena, Chen Rio,** and **Punta Chiquero**. Punta Morena is clearly marked and has a broad section of open beach. Chen Rio can be identified by a large rocky outcropping that forms a small protected bay. The largest restaurant on the east of the island is the **Naked Turtle**, located on a lovely crescent-shaped bay at Punta Chiquero.

At the south end of the island where the coast road turns west, there is a small cafe on **El Mirador Beach**. At this point, a dirt road turns off the main road, leading toward the **Point Celarain Lighthouse**. There is a long, beautiful beach here along the southeastern point of the island. The lighthouse is about 2¹/² miles (4 km) from the main road. For a beautiful view of this area, ask permission to climb to the top of the lighthouse.

EXPLORING THE YUCATAN PENINSULA

The Yucatan Peninsula juts to the northeast from the southern tail of the Mexican mainland. The peninsula is bordered on the north and west by the Gulf of Mexico, on the east by the Mexican Caribbean and on the south by Belize, Guatemala and the neighboring Mexican state of Tabasco. The Yucatan Peninsula is composed of three different states: Campeche on the west, Yucatan on the north, and Quintana Roo on the east.

With its beautiful beaches, lagoons and fabulous Mayan ruins, the peninsula has become an important drawing card for tourists.

Getting There

By boat. Passenger ferries depart regularly from the dock at the end of Avenida Benito Juarez in San Miguel. The new modern "water jet" boat, the *MV Mexico* holds many passengers in airline-style seats. The trip between Cozumel and Playa Del Carmen takes an average of one hour to one and one half hours. Cruise ships come and go from the International Pier which is located at the south end of hotel row across from the Fiesta Americana Sol Caribe Hotel. Car ferries depart the International Pier.

By air. There are several daily flights between Cozumel and Cancun, the newest and most modern international airport on the Yucatan Peninsula. The two main domestic airlines are AeroCaribe and AeroCozumel. Both provide regularly scheduled flights between Cozumel, and Cancun, Merida, Playa Del Carmen, Isla Mujeres, Chetumal, Chichen Itza and other destinations.

The Coast

The eastern coast of the state of Quintana Roo extends about 223 miles (360 km) from Cancun south to Chetumal. Throughout most of the year, the coastline resembles a tropical paradise of palm groves, low brush and mangroves. The jungle that lines the coast contains many lagoons and natural underground springs referred to as *cenotes*. Stretches of long sandy beaches alternate with rocky promontories, inlets and small protected bays. The waters are dotted with shallow coral reefs.

Cancun

The resort destination of Cancun is located near the northeast tip of the Yucatan Peninsula. In 20 years, it has exploded from a swampy area of land with a population of zero to a mega-bucks resort with nearly 200,000 people.

There are actually two different Cancuns. One is a long, slender island connected to the mainland by a bridge at each end. This island is literally lined with wall-to-wall highrise luxury hotels resembling massive, modern pyramids. Across the bridge at the northwest end of the "row" is Cancun City. Here, visitors will find moderately priced hotels and condominiums within walking distance of sidewalk cafes and a multitude of shops. There are a number of shallow reefs located a short distance from the hotels, but because of the run-off, the visibility is generally not very good.

Mescalito's is a popular bar on the east side of Cozumel, at the end of Cross Island Road.

The waterfront on Isla Mujeres is lined with boats of every size and description. Some are used for ferrying tourists back and forth to Cancun, while others are used for diving and fishing excursions.

Isla Mujeres

Isla Mujeres is a small island, approximately 5 miles (8 km) long and 1/2 mile (.8 km) wide, that lies 8 miles (13 km) across the Bay of Mujeres from Cancun and approximately 45 miles (73 km) north of Cozumel. The island is flat with large stretches of sandy beaches. There are fewer than 14,000 residents on the island, whose main town is a laid-back fishing village. Isla Mujeres has maintained its quaintness even though it has been discovered by tourists.

You can get there by plane or ferry. There are connecting flights from Cancun International Airport, as well as infrequent direct flights from Cozumel. AeroCaribe usually has three flights a week to Isla Mujeres, but the schedule is constantly changing.

There are two main ports where ferries leave from Cancun to Isla Mujeres. Puerto Juarez, located about 15 minutes north of downtown Cancun, is known as the "people ferry." This port has medium size ferries running at regular intervals throughout the day. Arrive at least 15 minutes earlier than the scheduled departure because the boats often leave a little early if they are full. You can also hire a small water taxi. These small boats are normally faster, however, depending on weather and water conditions, the ride can be wet and wild. There is also a "people and car" ferry that leaves from Punta Sam on a daily basis. The trip from Punta Sam is less frequent and longer.

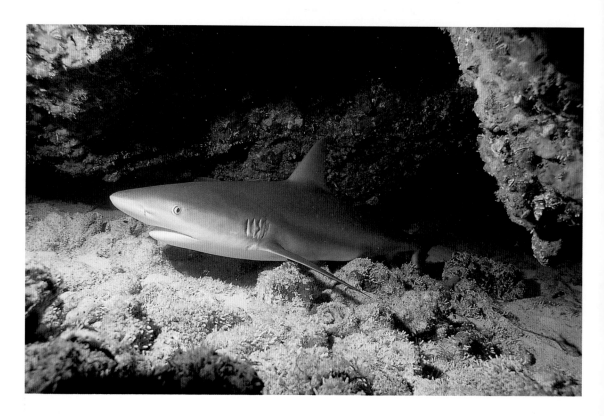

One of the attractions of diving from Isla Mujeres is the well-known "sleeping shark caves" on the northeast side of the island. Photo: Jesse Cancelmo.

If you plan on staying on the island for only the day, be sure to check the last departure time for the mainland.

There are a number of comfortable hotel accommodations on the island with a wide variety of prices. During peak tourist season, reservations are suggested. Isla Mujeres also has many excellent restaurants, sidewalk cafes, souvenir shops, fishing cruises, a market, banks, bakeries, pharmacies and dive shops.

You can also rent bicycles or hire taxis to get from one end of the island to the other. The town at the north end of the island is small enough to walk through unless you are hauling dive gear. The best beaches are **North Beach** on the northern end of the island near the town and **El Garrafon Beach** on the southern end of the island. El Garrafon offers the best snorkeling, but is often very crowded.

Isla Mujeres is the location of the well-known **sleeping shark caves** and also has some very interesting shallow dive sites. The caves of the sleeping sharks are located on the northeast side of the island and are accessible only when the ocean is calm. The various caves are between 50 and 70 feet (15-21 m) deep. Although the sharks are not always present, there is a good chance that divers will be able to see bull sharks, lemon sharks or gray reef sharks "sleeping" on floors of the caves.

Manchones Reef is a popular shallow reef on the southwest side of Isla Mujeres, off El Garrafon Beach. This large site offers a series of coral ridges in depths between 20 and 40 feet (6-12 m). The tops of the ridges are lined with elkhorn coral, and divers can expect to encounter large schools of grunts, snapper and goatfish hovering above sections of the reef.

The tops of many of the reefs near Isla Mujeres, including Manchones, are lined with beautiful growths of elkhorn coral.

Isla Contoy

An interesting side trip from Isla Mujeres is Isla Contoy, a bird sanctuary located about a 45-minute boat ride north of Isla Mujeres. The island is deserted, except for many varieties of exotic birds, a government owned museum and a lighthouse. The island also offers excellent snorkeling.

Archaeological Sites

One of the most popular archeological sites on the mainland is **Tulum**, located about 15 miles (25 km) south of **Akumal** on coastal highway 307. A side road leads to the ruins that cover an area 180 yards (165 m) by 435 yards (398 m). There are approximately 60 well-preserved stone structures at Tulum, which are perched atop a cliff overlooking the ocean. This is the largest fortified site on the Quintana Roo coastline.

There is a picturesque sandy beach situated below the cliffs offering a place for a refreshing swim after a tour of the ruins. Many divers who come to Cozumel for a week trip take a day excursion to Tulum. The tour can be arranged through your resort on Cozumel. Most people take the ferry, hydro-plane or travel by air to Playa Del Carmen and then continue on by

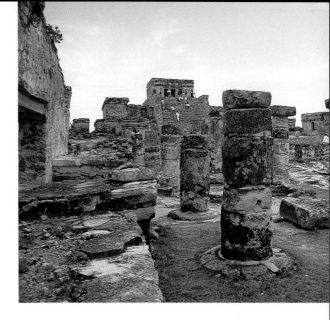

Tulum, meaning "wall" in Mayan, is a relatively small site measuring approximately 1255 feet (380 m) by 545 feet (165 m). Tulum was part of a series of coastal forts established between A.D. 700 and A.D. 1000. Photo: Phil Zarri.

Chichen-Itza exhibits a mingling of
Mayan and Toltec architecture, and
is perhaps the most popular
destination of its type on the Yucatan
Peninsula. Photo: Phil Zarri.

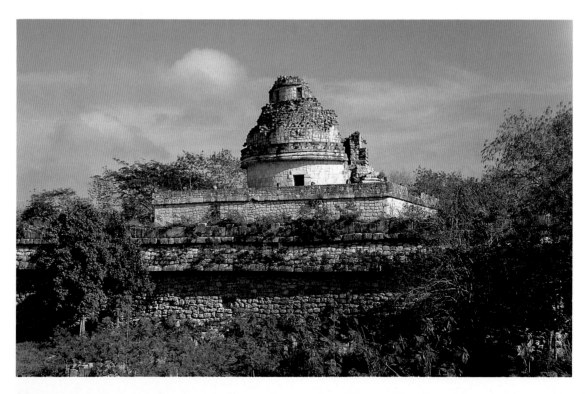

guided taxi or bus tour. After a guided tour of Tulum, be sure to visit the natural lagoon of **Xel-Ha** for some snorkeling before continuing on to the beach resort at Akumal for a late lunch. Xel-Ha (pronounced shell-haah), has a beautiful lagoon that consists of a mix of fresh and salt water inhabited by some rare tropical fishes. The lagoon is now a national park and is protected from fishing.

The extensive ruins of **Chichen-Itza** are now only a one hour plane ride from Cozumel on AeroCaribe or AeroCozumel. The aerial view of the main pyramid and the lush green jungle is very impressive. This is the most famous of the ancient Mayan cities. The earliest buildings date back to A.D. 600. While most of the buildings are Mayan, those dating from the 10th century include a Toltec influence, resulting from the Toltec invasion which began around A.D. 950.

Among the most interesting features of the ruins at Chichen-Itza are the 75-foot high pyramid (a temple to Quetzalcoatl, named Kukulkan by the Mayans), the ritual ball courts where the winners were sacrificed, the El Characol observatory, and the reclining figure of Chacmool.

Coba is a site which dates back to the classic Mayan period. It is set among several lakes located inland from the coast about 60 miles southwest of Cancun. This area was never discovered by the Spaniards and consequently has been found in an unspoiled condition. It is currently undergoing restoration. The site covers an immense area of more than 19 square miles (50 sq km) and hundreds of mounds are yet to be cleared and uncovered. Nohoch Mul, which towers 12 stories above the ground and is the tallest pyramid on the Yucatan Peninsula, offers an excellent (and dizzying) view of the surrounding jungle and the remainder of Coba.

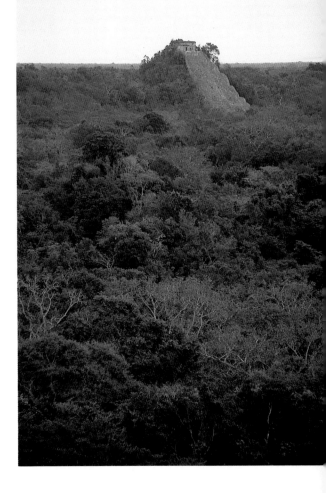

Coba is an inland site that was never discovered by the Spaniards. Photo: Phil Zarri.

One of the most interesting and graceful structures at Chichen-Itza is Caracol, the observatory. Photo: Phil Zarri.

CHAPTER **V**   DIVING

Almost all diving in Cozumel is done along the leeward western shore of the island. Although reefs nearly encircle Cozumel, the windward eastern shore is continuously pounded by heavy wave action, making it dangerous for sport diving. The western side of the island is normally protected from the prevailing tradewinds. With the exception of north-northwest winds that frequently blow during the late fall and sometimes during the early winter, the sea on Cozumel's western side is normally calm.

All divers coming to Cozumel are strongly urged to visit the **Museo De La Isla De Cozumel** (The Museum of the Island of Cozumel) where you will find a wealth of information about the reef formations, natural history, Mayan culture and contemporary history. A visit to the museum will make you more aware of the need to practice environmentally sound diving.

SHORE DIVING

There are many areas teeming with interesting marine life that can be easily reached from shore. These sites provide inexpensive dives to supplement the wide assortment of boat dive packages offered on the island.

Except in unusually rough conditions, the shore dives listed here offer easy entries and exits. Access is generally over sandy beaches or down stairways cut into the ironshore. All of the shoreline in Cozumel is open to the public. This includes access to the water in front of hotels. With your C-card, you can rent a tank and then take a taxi with all your equipment to the dive site. You may be able to arrange in advance to have a tank waiting for you, as there are dive operations at all of the entry points listed in this book as shore dive sites.

Even those hotels that don't have a reef close to shore have excellent shore diving opportunities. At the **Club Cozumel Caribe**, one of the northernmost hotels on the island, divers can scuba or snorkel at night just off the hotel pier with dozens of large, silvery tarpon. The tarpon come in to feed on schools of baitfish that are attracted by powerful lights directed into the water. Tires and other manmade items placed offshore at the **Galapago Inn** offer a great place to look for octopus, eels, trunkfish, hermit crabs and a variety of other nocturnal feeders. This makes an especially good night dive location.

BOAT DIVING

There are a wide variety of dive boats operating in Cozumel. Eight to ten years ago, almost all of the dive boats were the slow "motor-sailers." These boats often took hours to reach the southernmost reefs, making a two-tank boat trip a whole day affair. Today, however, almost all of the dive operations use fast boats, most of which are equipped with heavy-duty twin outboard motors. These boats usually leave the dock at 9:00 A.M. for a two-tank boat trip and return between 11:30 A.M. and 1:00 P.M. depending upon the location of your hotel and distance to the sites. With the faster boats, resorts on the north side of town can also run half-day trips to the south. In peak season and whenever there is sufficient demand, many of the dive resorts will run two-tank trips in the afternoon as well as the morning.

Flamingo tongue cowries can often be found grazing on the stalks of gorgonian sea fans. The decorative spots are actually part of a retractable mantle.

Fast boats make the trip to the reefs quickly, allowing divers to take a two-tank trip and be back at the hotel in time for lunch.

Divers wait to be picked up after a drift dive. Almost all dives on Cozumel are conducted as drift dives because of the current.

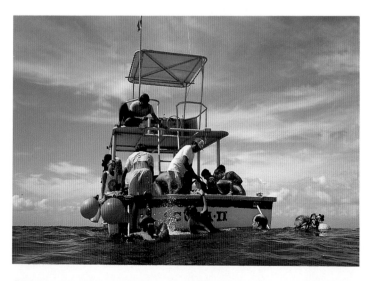

Divers await their turn to clamber back into the boat at the end of an enjoyable dive.

Resorts that book week-long dive packages will try to keep the same group of divers together throughout the course of the week so that everyone will get to see as many different reefs as possible. It is also standard practice that the less difficult dives are made in the beginning of the week and the more experienced dive sites later in the week. In this way, divers are given a chance to become familiar with drift diving, and the guides get a chance to determine individual skill levels within the groups.

Of course, there a large number of independent dive operators with smaller, fast boats. Most of these operations have boats that hold six to eight divers. They are an excellent choice for small groups because they can cater to the group's specific desires. Groups of experienced divers may want to set up trips with operations like **Dive Paradise** or **Deportes Acuaticos** where they can arrange to go only to the more exciting, advanced dives. Other groups may wish to elect to dive reefs which require only intermediate skill levels.

Drift Diving

Almost all boat diving in Cozumel is drift diving. The Guiana Current that runs in a northly direction sweeps up to the southern end of the island, producing currents of variable strength. These currents are almost always present and tend to run from south to north. Currents often change in intensity and even direction during the course of a dive, necessitating experienced dive guides as well as boat captains.

Once the boat reaches the dive site and divers are geared up, the dive guide will give a short description of the site and outline the dive plan, including depth and time. All divers leave the boat at the same time and meet the guide on the sand bottom next to the reef.

As soon as everyone is ready, the divers move off in the same directon as the current. Most of the time, the current is less than half a knot, but occasionally currents can be quite strong, sometimes reaching two knots or more. When you get used to drift diving, you will find that this type of diving is almost effortless. You use your buoyancy control to stay off the bottom and just drift along the reef using the current to carry you along. As the divers drift

with the current below the surface of the water, the "live boat" follows the group's bubbles.

Most of the dive guides will allow buddy teams to do their own thing as long as they have demonstrated they are competent divers and they adhere to the depth limit set by the guide. When divers reach a designated minimum tank pressure, they ascend to the surface and wait for the boat to pick them up. Unless there is a strong current, divers may do a "drift" safety stop at 15 feet (5 m). If you are uncomfortable making a safety stop while drifting, be more conservative with your bottom time. I recommend that a signal device such as a bright orange inflatable safety sausage be carried by each diver.

Currents and Coral

The dominant current flowing through the Caribbean originates in the South Atlantic. When the current reaches the Brazilian bulge it splits. About 40 percent of the flow moves along the north face of South America and into the Caribbean Sea. This flow is called the Guiana Current. Because the earth's rotation causes currents to bend clockwise in the northern hemisphere, the Guiana is flowing almost due north as it sweeps around Cozumel.

This large volume of water is severely constricted as it flows through the narrow Yucatan Channel which spans about 100 miles (170 km) between Mexico and Cuba. This constriction results in the current reaching speeds of over 2 knots in the Channel and as much as 8 knots between Cozumel and the mainland.

Corals thrive in strong current which constantly delivers oxygenated and carbonated water to support their metabolism, and at the same time, sweeps away fouling sediments. The most massive coral formations on Cozumel lie off the south shore which faces the current.

The excellent water clarity found in Cozumel enhances the amount of sunlight penetrating the water, thus increasing coral calcification and growth.

Because much of Cozumel is made up of porous materials such as ironshore, rain water rapidly percolates into the ground and travels to the sea through subterranean channels. This lack of rivers and runoff prevents fouling of the reefs.

As currents bend around the west side of Cozumel, a small, clockwise eddy sometimes forms. This temporary condition causes a southward current near the shore, usually between San Miguel and Punta Tormentos. A more permanent eddy persists on the northern side of the island. Some of the water which has swept up to the north becomes caught in these spiral circulations and rapidly slows down. Fine sediment and coral debris that was suspended in the formerly fast moving current settles to the bottom producing a flat, marshy shore with mangroves and a large, shallow sand bank.

The northeasterly trade winds, which cool off the afternoons, also cause the predominant wave swell out of the northeast. Since Cuba acts as a breakwater, the wave action striking Cozumel is moderate. The sandy bottom on the east coast is stirred up by frequent wave action which smothers significant coral growth. However, tubeworms and coralline algae have constructed a few large, cemented reef formations here. The wave action is also sufficient to create a littoral drift along the shore, which transports sand from the north depositing it along the eastern shore. This flow of sand produces the east coast beaches and the sand bank on the south end of Cozumel which terminates with sand falls dropping off between the giant buttresses of the southern reefs.

EQUIPMENT

There are several large dive stores in addition to quite a number of small operations on Cozumel. Good rental gear can be obtained from most reputable shops. However, I recommend that divers should have their own mask, regulator, buoyancy compensator and gauges whenever traveling abroad.

MARINE LIFE PRESERVATION

The Cozumel Association of Dive Operators (CADO) has developed a list of basic diving guidelines in order to preserve the marine life.

- On boat dives, all divers descend onto sandy areas adjacent to the reefs, and not directly on top of corals. This allows divers to adjust their buoyancy without damaging any coral.
- Divers should attain neutral buoyancy before swimming over reefs.
- Divemasters and instructors are encouraged to do what they can to get divers to minimize the amount of weight they wear.
- Any gear that might drag along the surface of the reef such as dangling gauges or octopus regulators should be secured.
- Divers should stay at least three feet away from corals, sponges and other delicate animals.
- No marine animals should be collected. Within the National Marine Park, it is against the law to take corals, sponges, shells, or other marine life. All of the dive sites detailed in this book, except for Barracuda and San Juan Reefs, lie within the National Marine Park.

At night, divers will often see basket stars perched atop coral heads, sea fans or whip corals. Basket stars feed at night and hide in the reef during the day.

All reputable operators require divers to hang at 15 feet for a three-minute safety stop at the end of every dive.

SAFETY

In recent years, the diving practices in Cozumel have come under a great deal of scrutiny. Operations have been criticized for not adhering to safe diving practices, for accepting unqualified divers, and for taking divers on dives that are well beyond their skill levels.

Over the last 12 years, I have made hundreds of dives on the island and have become familiar with most of the dive operations. Although I have heard several stories about unsafe dive operations, I have personally never experienced any, with the possible exception of marginally short surface intervals between multiple dives.

Since the Cozumel Association of Dive Operators (CADO) was formed in the late 1980's, there has been an even greater emphasis on safety. Divers can expect the following procedures by CADO members:

- When divers check in, they must present their C-cards, and in some cases their log books.
- Operators will often conduct a shallow water checkout dive to evaluate a diver's capabilities and to allow each diver to check his or her gear.
- Divers completing only a resort course will be limited to a maximum depth of 40 feet (12 m).
- The more difficult dives will be done near the end of the vacation so divers have a chance to "work up" to those dives.
- Deep dives are always the first dive of the day and are usually limited to depths of 80 or 90 feet (24 or 27 m). Advanced divers with more experience are permitted to go on some deeper dives in more remote areas.
- Second dives on a two-tank dive trip are made in depths shallower than 60 feet (18 m) after an appropriate surface interval.
- Divers are encouraged to take a minimum three-minute safety stop at 15 feet (3 m) after every dive.
- Most operations provide one divemaster for groups up to ten, and two divemasters for groups of more than ten.

UNDERWATER TERRAIN

Cozumel is oriented along a north/south axis. A drop-off roughly parallels the western shoreline from Punte Norte at the northwest corner of the island to Punta Celarain at the south end of the island. Most of the reefs are located at the lip of this drop-off, or parallel to the drop-off at a variety of depths. The reefs can be roughly categorized according to their depths as either shallow, mid-depth or deep reefs, although the bottom contours and reef types vary greatly. The depths of the reefs and the intensity of the currents dictate whether they are considered as novice, intermediate or advanced sites.

There is a tremendous variety of corals in Cozumel. Purple and pink gorgonian fans are found in great numbers in the shallow areas where there is considerable wave action. Brain corals, whip corals and lettuce corals are commonly seen as a patchwork of color on most mid-depth reefs. On deeper reefs and on the wall dives, there are huge tube sponges, tangles of rope sponge, black coral and large deep water gorgonians.

A photographer, looking for small schools of fish, explores an overhang at La Francesa.

VISIBILITY

The underwater visibility in Cozumel is usually the best that can be found in the entire Caribbean, averaging 150 feet (45 m) year-round and often reaching 200 feet (61 m) or more. This extreme clarity sometimes makes it possible for boat captains to actually see the divers as they swim along the bottom.

WATER TEMPERATURE

The waters around Cozumel are warm all year. The temperature varies from a low of 77°F (25°C) in the winter and a high of 84°F (29°C) in the late summer months. While a dive skin is sufficient protection from cuts, scrapes and abrasions during the warmer months, it is a good idea to wear a 1/8 inch (3 mm) wet suit for extra warmth from November through March.

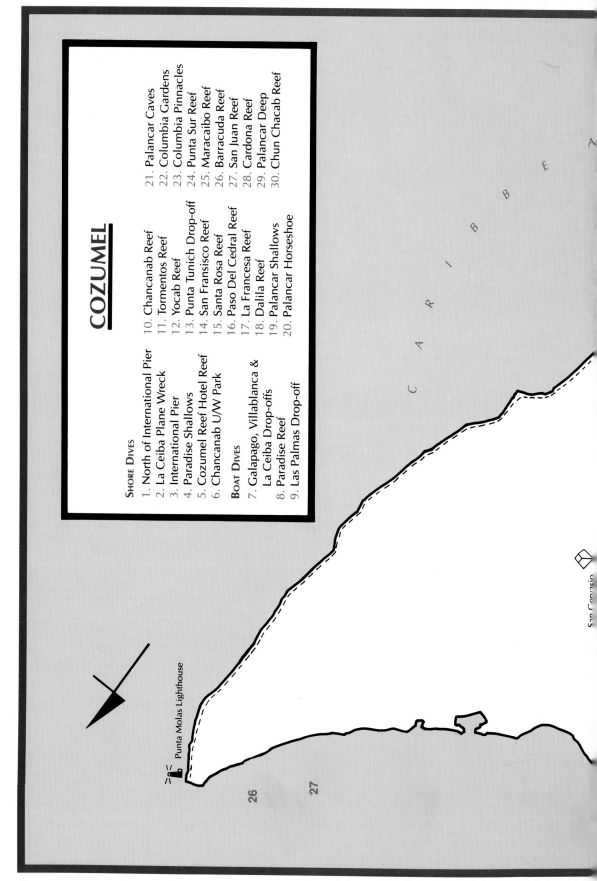

COZUMEL

SHORE DIVES

1. North of International Pier
2. La Ceiba Plane Wreck
3. International Pier
4. Paradise Shallows
5. Cozumel Reef Hotel Reef
6. Chancanab U/W Park

BOAT DIVES

7. Galapago, Villablanca &
   La Ceiba Drop-offs
8. Paradise Reef
9. Las Palmas Drop-off

10. Chancanab Reef
11. Tormentos Reef
12. Yocab Reef
13. Punta Tunich Drop-off
14. San Fransisco Reef
15. Santa Rosa Reef
16. Paso Del Cedral Reef
17. La Francesa Reef
18. Dalila Reef
19. Palancar Shallows
20. Palancar Horseshoe

21. Palancar Caves
22. Columbia Gardens
23. Columbia Pinnacles
24. Punta Sur Reef
25. Maracaibo Reef
26. Barracuda Reef
27. San Juan Reef
28. Cardona Reef
29. Palancar Deep
30. Chun Chacab Reef

Punta Molas Lighthouse

CARIBBEA

San Gervasio

26

27

S E A

Punta Morena Beach

Chen Rio Beach

Punta Chiqueros Beach

El Mirador Beach

Tumba del Caracol

Punta Celarain Lighthouse

Laguna Ciolumba

Shore Road

San Fransisco Beach

El Cedral

Chancanab National Park

Caleta Harbor

International Pier

San Miguel

Passenger Ferry

Cross Island Road

Airport

1 7 3 2
5 4
8
9 10
6
11
12
13
28
14 16
15
17 18
20
21 19
29
22 23
24
25
30

Florida

Cuba

Cayman Islands

Caribbean Sea

Gulf of Mexico

Yucatan Channel

Mexico

Cozumel

CHAPTER **VI**   DIVE SITES

SHORE DIVING

1. NORTH OF INTERNATIONAL PIER

DEPTH: 15-25 FEET

(5-8 M)

CURRENT: LIGHT

A shallow reef runs roughly parallel to the shoreline, beginning about a mile (1.6 km) north of San Miguel. This reef, which consists of small coral heads, and scattered gorgonians and sea whips, lies close to shore.

The first section begins in front of the La Perla Hotel. The second section, divided from the first by a wide open stretch of sand, is laid out in a continous string of scattered coral heads from the Villablanca Hotel south to the International Pier. Most of the coral heads are between 15 and 25 feet (5-8 m) deep. Different sections of this reef can be accessed from the La Perla Hotel, the pier across the street from the Villablanca Hotel, the piers across the street from the Casa Del Mar and Sol Caribe Hotels, the Sol Caribe lagoon and from the La Ceiba Hotel pier.

2. LA CEIBA PLANE WRECK

DEPTH: 35 FEET

(11 M)

CURRENT: NONE TO

MODERATE

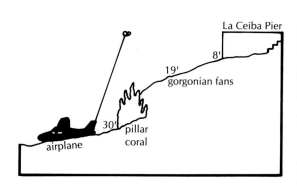

In 1977, a 40-passenger, twin engine DC3 was purposely sunk as a prop for a Mexican disaster film. The owners of the La Ceiba Hotel saved the plane to be used as an artificial reef and dive site just off the hotel. In recent years, the plane wreck has been overturned, damaged and moved during various storms. It now rests in 35 feet (11 m) of water, about 65 yards (60 m) offshore. There is a small white buoy that marks the location, straight out from the end of the dive shop pier at the La Ceiba Hotel.

Beautiful sponges grow along the vertical wall at the north end of Santa Rosa Reef.

The wreckage of an old DC-3 now lies in 35 feet of water, about 60 yards off the end of the La Ceiba Dive Shop Pier. This area makes a great day dive as well as a great night dive spot.

Access to the site can be gained through the La Ceiba Hotel. If you're staying at another hotel or resort, you can take a taxi to the La Ceiba. Just throw your dive gear in the trunk. It's a good idea to take a towel along to dry off after the dive and to sit on during the return taxi ride. You can walk through the lobby to get to the walkway along the water's edge. There are two main access points to the water along this walkway, one set of stairs near the hotel pool and the other next to the dive shop pier. The easiest entry into the water is a giant stride off the end of the pier. Other access points are located at the Sol Caribe Hotel lagoon and the second Del Mar Aquatics pier across the street from the Casa Del Mar Hotel.

There is rarely much wave chop or heavy current here because the plane sits in a protected "V" between the shoreline and the International Pier. The wreck itself sits on a flat sandy bottom.

During the day, the remains of the plane give refuge to large schools of grunts, snapper and a variety of reef fishes. An assortment of anemones, small shrimp and arrow crabs can be found clinging to parts of the wreckage.

The flat sandy area abuts against a steep slope on the shore side of the plane. Here, the bottom rises quickly to between 15 and 20 feet (5-6 m) and then levels off. From the top edge of this slope, the bottom rises gradually to the shoreline. There are many purple gorgonian fans scattered around the coral heads in this shallow area. Flamingo tongue cowries, with their striking spotted mantles, can be found on most of these fans. Divers will also find hundreds of Christmas tree tube worms protruding from the corals, as well as hermit crabs, mantis shrimp, and tiny blennies. As an added treat, divers have recently begun to find sea horses in this area. All of these tiny animals offer excellent subjects for macro photography and video.

The area along the steep slope is crowded with large coral heads, including some impressive pinnacles of pillar coral. This shallow reef, consisting of numerous coral heads extends to the north and south along the shore. Look closely for cleaning stations with juvenile Spanish hogfish.

Excellent night dive. The shallows around the plane wreck offer an excellent night dive location. When you enter the water, get your bearings on the set of lights that are located near your exit point. The La Ceiba pier has one green and one red light.

The scattered coral heads around the plane are teeming with life at night. The schools of grunts that hide in the wreckage during the day disperse over the sandy bottom to forage for food. Spiny lobsters and slipper lobsters are very common in this area, as are octopus and eels. For serious photographers and videographers, this area is superb at night. There is little or no current, and with the shallow depth, bottom time is almost unlimited.

3. INTERNATIONAL PIER

DEPTH:	20-30 FEET
	(6-9 M)
CURRENT:	LIGHT TO
	MODERATE

As with most piers, the pilings have a great deal of growth, and the bottom around the pilings is littered with rubble and assorted man-made materials.

The rubble on the bottom comes to life at night, making this an interesting place for close-up and macro photography, and video. The pilings and rubble are covered with colorful encrusting sponges and corals. Look for orange ball anemones, hermit crabs, splendid toadfish, yellow stingrays, rough file clams, balloonfish, moray eels and a variety of other interesting marine life. In the water column around the pilings, divers will often find schools of small jacks, barracuda and squid.

Caution. Because of the comings and goings of large cruise ships and other ferry boats, this area can be dangerous. On weekends, there are usually no cruise ships docked at the pier, but one or more are almost always present during weekdays. Also, the car ferry makes frequent trips between this pier and Playa Del Carmen on the mainland. There is considerable danger from the huge props on these ships, which cause strong suction and turbulence. If you are bent on diving this area, you should check with the harbor master to obtain a schedule of times when the area will be free of ships.

4. PARADISE SHALLOWS

DEPTH:	20 FEET
	(6 M)
CURRENT:	LIGHT

Paradise Shallows, also known as Caleta Reef, is a continuation of the patch reef that runs from the La Perla to the International Pier.

This site consists of widely scattered coral heads, sponges and other corals, such as sea whips and sea fans. It continues south, paralleling the shoreline, from the International Pier to Caleta Lagoon. Paradise Shallows is situated between the shore and Paradise (Paraiso) Reef. Depth averages 20 feet (6 m).

When the current is running from south to north, as it usually does, it is possible to swim out to Paradise Shallows from shore. There are lots of exit points as you drift toward the north, including the International Pier and several hotel piers just beyond. When making a shore dive, it is a good idea to take a small waterproof container with sufficient money for the return taxi ride and perhaps some refreshments at the end of the dive.

5. COZUMEL REEF HOTEL REEF

DEPTH:	20 FEET
	(6 M)
CURRENT:	LIGHT

This shallow site is close to shore and easily accessible from the Beach Club located across the street from the Cozumel Reef Hotel (Holiday Inn). Although this area suffered extreme damage from the 1988 hurricane, there is a dramatic amount of new coral and sponge growth on the gently sloping bottom. A variety of reef fishes and other marine life can be seen here.

6. CHANCANAB UNDERWATER PARK

DEPTH:	15-35 FEET
	(5-11 M)
CURRENT:	NONE TO LIGHT

The Chancanab Underwater Park, often spelled Chancanaab, is probably the most popular and well known shore dive on Cozumel. The name means "little ocean" and comes from the picturesque lagoon at the Park. The lagoon, now only a few feet deep, used to be connected to the ocean by a short tunnel through which divers could swim. That tunnel is now closed off, and the lagoon is off limits to everyone. There are a couple of wooden observation platforms that have been built next to the lagoon for fish watching in this outdoor, natural aquarium.

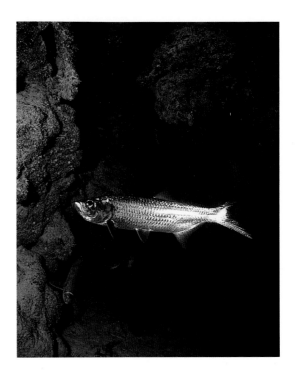

Large silvery tarpon cruise about the recesses of the caves at Chancanab.

The Chancanab National Underwater Park offers a wide variety of activities including sunbathing, snorkeling and scuba diving.

A huge school of friendly snapper hang out at a huge coral head just offshore from the access steps at Chancanab.

On the northern edge of the Park, there is a shallow, protected sandy cove where swimming is permitted. It is perfect for young children and toddlers. This cove even has a small shipwreck equipped with a water slide.

There are extensive facilities located at the Park including several gift stores and boutiques, a beautifully manicured botanical garden, and an interesting museum which explains the history of Chancanab. Of course, there is also a fully equipped dive store, a restaurant and fresh water showers to rinse off the sand. Chancanab is an excellent place to spend a whole day diving, snorkeling, sunning, eating and taking a leisurely stroll on the shaded pathways.

The Park police are very serious about enforcing the restrictions against the use of knives or even wearing gloves inside the waters that are part of the National Park.

On the oceanside of the Park, there are steps and railings which assist divers, snorkelers and swimmers getting in and out of the water. The coral and rocky surfaces in the shallows are covered with multi-colored Christmas tree tube worms. There are several high profile coral heads about 25 yards (23 m) offshore. At one particularly large coral head directly offshore from the steps at the main part of the Park, a large school of friendly snapper can usually be found in only 20 to 30 feet (6-9 m) of water. This is an excellent place to snorkel or have an orientation scuba dive.

For divers with more experience, there are two sets of caves which actually penetrate back under the shoreline. Diving depths range from 15 to 35 feet (5-11 m). The first cave is located near one of the stairways into the water. Divers will also find the entrance to an extensive system of caves about 75 yards (68 m) to the south of the main Park. There are several wide entrances and exits to a large cavern that has tunnels heading off in many different directions. This system of caves has been explored by expert cave divers for a distance of over 1,650 yards (1,500 m) into the interior of the island.

Caution. Cave diving requires special training and equipment. **Do not** leave the cavern (natural light) zone unless you are a certified cave diver with the proper cave diving equipment.

To find the entrance to the caves, follow the shore line closely until you see a large cut or channel. The caves are located on the Park side of this cut. In the outer cavern, it is common to find large tarpon and swarms of small, silvery baitfish floating through large underwater chambers. Some people refer to this area as Beachcomber Cavern, reputedly named after a restaurant that used to sit beside the cut when the old road passed directly along the shoreline. The road has since been moved inland so that it doesn't interfere with the ecology or detract from the esthetics of the Park.

BOAT DIVING

7. THE GALAPAGO, VILLABLANCA & LA CEIBA DROP-OFFS

DEPTH:	15-100+ FEET
	(5-30+ M)
CURRENT:	MODERATE TO
	STRONG

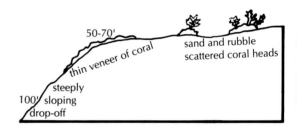

These three drop-offs are actually different sections of the continuous wall that runs along the entire west coast of Cozumel 200 to 400 yards (182-364 m) offshore. A mostly sandy bottom, dotted with coral heads, gorgonian fans and large sponges, slopes gently from the shore to the edge of the drop-offs which begin at depths between 50 and 70 feet (15-21 m). While the wall is fairly steep in most places, some areas are nearly vertical. The lip of the wall from the Galapago Inn Resort to the La Ceiba Hotel runs roughly parallel to shore and

The lip of the drop-off at the Galapago Wall is dotted with red sponges and deep-water gorgonian fans.

The La Ceiba Drop-off has a large number of huge, brown tub sponges.

Splendid toadfish, one of the unique varieties of marine life in Cozumel are usually seen peering out from under ledges.

is several hundred yards off the beach.

These sites are rarely visited because of their close proximity to the major hotels. In addition, there is not as much coral buildup on the lip of the drop-off as there is at some of the more popular reefs further to the south.

Because the currents are frequently strong in this area, there is a good chance to see schools of baitfish, bar jacks, horse-eye jacks and large pelagics such as barracuda, grouper and an occasional ray or shark. These sites are not recommended as beach dives because of the distances from shore, the depths and the potential for very strong currents.

8. PARADISE REEF

DEPTH:	22-40 FEET
	(7-12 M)
CURRENT:	LIGHT TO
	MODERATE

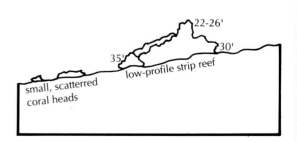

Paradise (Paraiso) Reef consists of five separate ridges, lined up roughly end to end and running parallel to shore. The reef begins about 150 to 200 yards (136-182 m) straight out from the entrance to the Celeta Lagoon located on the north side of the Stouffer El Presidente Hotel. It continues on toward the International Pier. The ridges rise only 5 to 10 feet (2-3 m) above a flat sandy bottom and are 25 to 40 yards (23-36 m) wide in most places. There are a few solitary, lofty pinnacles in the center of the reef. The maximum depth here is 40 feet.

The currents at Paradise Reef are light to moderate, and usually run south to north toward the International Pier. While there are few caves and tunnels within the reef structures, there are a myriad of cracks, crevices and overhangs on either side of the reef. The terrain is not spectacular, but the marine life is varied and abundant.

Keep in mind when you are diving this area that the reef sections are not lined up exactly end to end. There is a wide sand channel between the largest sections of the reef, and in one area you must swim diagonally to your left to find the beginning of the next section of reef.

Splendid toadfish. Paradise Reef is one of the best places to find Cozumel's toadfish, which goes by the common names of "Cozumel catfish" or "splendid toadfish." This unusual animal can usually be found peeking out from low ledges on the sand bottom on either side of the reef. The toadfish has a wide, compressed head with whisker-like appendages extending from the underside of its mouth. It has horizontal white and charcoal-blue, gray stripes on its head and body, with all of its fins lined in bright yellow.

Small schools of grunt and snapper can be found tucked into the cuts and crevices in the reef, or grouped around the prevalent whip corals. Feeding stations with juvenile hogfish and cleaner wrasse can be found everywhere.

Gorgonian sea fans provide food and shelter to a variety of beautiful and interesting animals including flamingo tongue cowries.

Orange filefish, cowfish, scrawled filefish, grouper and various types of parrotfishes are among the most common fishes on the reef. It is also a good place to see spotted moray eels, which will often swim out of the reef during the day. Don't extend your fingers in front of the eels. Some are used to being fed, and the combination of a good appetite.and poor eyesight can lead them to mistake your fingers for a handout.

The reef has lots of small vase sponges and a wonderful variety of anemones. For macro photography, there are many small animals including hermit crabs, banded shrimp, arrow crabs, Christmas tree tube worms and bristle worms.

Because of its location and depth, this site is usually visited as a shallow second dive after a deeper wall dive.

Popular night dive. Paradise is the most popular site for boat night diving. Divers will almost always be treated to appearances by octopuses, toadfish, eels, puffers, trunkfish and a variety of sleeping reef fishes.

9. LAS PALMAS DROP-OFF

DEPTH:	50-100+ FEET
	(15-30+ M)
CURRENT:	MODERATE TO
	STRONG

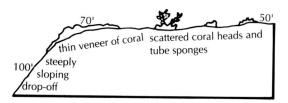

The Las Palmas drop-off is named after two tall, lonely looking palm trees which stand by themselves just on the north side of the Cozumel Reef Hotel (Holiday Inn). The sand and rubble bottom slopes gently downward to the top of the drop-off in approximately 70 feet (21 m) of water. The currents usually run from south to north along this reef and are often quite strong.

The lip of the drop-off is dotted with large deep-water gorgonian fans, enormous basket sponges and large coral heads. At this site, it is often fairly easy to video and photograph some of the more skittish varieties of fish such as queen angels. This is because there aren't many caves and crevices for them to dart into, and they seem reluctant to leave the shelter of their adopted coral head. Above the reef, in the water column, divers will frequently see schools of silvery baitfish and rainbow runners, often closely pursued by large jacks or barracuda.

The wall itelf is very steep in most places. Pairs of large angelfishes, shy squirrelfishes, and small reef fishes are common here. The deeper you go along this wall, the greater are the chances you will see large pelagics.

10. CHANCANAB REEF

DEPTH:	35-50 FEET
	(11-17 M)
CURRENT:	MODERATE

Chancanab Reef lies several hundred meters offshore just south of the Park at Chancanab Lagoon. The reef has two distinct sections separated by a wide sand and rubble channel.

North Section

The northern section is a high profile strip reef with many cuts, tunnels, overhangs and caves. This section sits on a fairly flat sand and rubble bottom with an average depth of 50 feet (15 m). The ridge rises to within 35 feet (11 m) of the surface.

Huge lobsters. The northern area has lots of huge, spiny lobsters (two varieties), some

A banded shrimp forages for food on the branches of a deep-water gorgonian.

BLACK CORAL

Black coral is a member of the gorgonian family, and is usually found only in areas where there is little light and strong currents. Black coral reproduces itself by a larva, which is negatively phototoxic, so it seeks out dark areas to grow. In shallower depths, black coral is found in caves and caverns. It is also found in the open on deep vertical walls, where little light penetrates. When viewed underwater with a dive light, branches of black coral appear orange-brown to orange-red.

Among the characteristics that add value to the black coral are the veins in the center of the stalks which represent different stages of growth. Accumulations of calcium are accentuated with brownish and reddish tones.

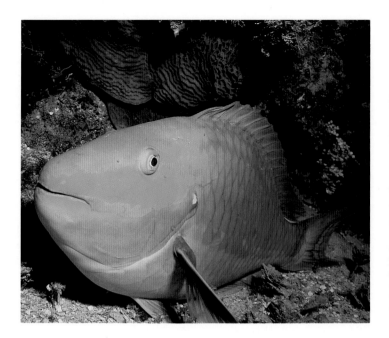

Chancanab Reef is one of the two most popular boat night dives on Cozumel. Fishes, such as this parrotfish, can be approached easily at night.

weighing over 20 pounds (9 kg). This is also an excellent area to observe juvenile hogfish pick parasites from various reef fish that wait patiently in line to be cleaned. Black grouper are also fairly common here. In addition, there are lots of bright yellow, red, orange and flourescent purple sponges.

The ridge section is honey-combed with a maze of tunnels and caves that teem with marine life. Divers will encounter lobsters and crabs as well as assorted bigeye and glasseye squirrelfish, large porgies, and small schools of margates and grunts.

South Section

The second section, at the south end, consists of a patch reef made up of broken sections of ridges, ending in a scattering of large coral heads. This section is a bit shallower than the north end, with the bottom ranging between 40 and 45 feet (12-14 m).

Good night dive. This is a popular night boat dive location. At night you will find the lobsters out on top of the reef. There is also an abundance of toadfish, eels, puffers, octopuses and sleeping fishes. One unusual sight to look for is a sleeping parrotfish which has enveloped itself in a protective cocoon.

11. TORMENTOS REEF

DEPTH:	30-70 FEET
	(9-21 M)
CURRENT:	LIGHT TO
	STRONG

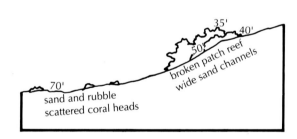

35'
40'
50'
broken patch reef
wide sand channels
70'
sand and rubble
scattered coral heads

Tormentos Reef is a broken patch reef that protrudes from a sloping, sandy bottom. The reef is located directly out from Punta Tormentos and slightly to the south of Chancanab Reef. It is named after Punta Tormentos, although sometimes you would swear that the reef was so named because of the torrential current which frequently scours the reef.

The south end of the reef begins about 50 yards (46 m) to the north of the end of Yocab Reef across a barren, sandy gap. At this end, the slope begins on a flat sand and rubble bottom in about 30 feet (9 m) of water and drops quickly to a depth of about 60 feet (18 m). It then gradually levels off at 70 feet (21 m) as you get farther from the reef heading toward the drop-off.

Most of the exposed reef structure is between 30 and 60 feet (9-18 m) deep, from the tops of the coral heads to the base of the reef sections. The reef angles toward the northwest so that the north end of the reef reaches a depth of about 70 feet (21 m), and is closer to the drop-off than the southern end.

The majority of the individual sections of the reef extend out across the downward slope making them much higher off the bottom on the offshore side. There are approximately 50 to 70 individual sections of this reef scattered across the sand bottom. The top of the reef is as shallow as 30 feet (9 m) in some areas, so it usually makes a good site for the second dive of the day.

The reef is decorated with whip corals, brain corals and a wide variety of colorful sponges. When the current is light, you can get excellent photographs along the top of the reef where there are innumerable small invertebrates such as flamingo tongue cowries, arrow crabs, banded shrimp, coral shrimp, delicate brittle stars and crinoids. Work with the dive guides to find good locations for pictures. Then set up a shot and wait for your subjects to cruise through the scene.

When the current is strong, it is a good place to drift along taking wide-angle video of groupers and solitary barracuda which hang out in the current. Chubs and yellowtail snapper are obviously used to being fed in this area and will usually cluster around visiting divers. Schools of creole wrasse are also common. This is a good area for getting stills or video of swarms of fish hanging around divers. When taking videos of fish-feeding scenes (when feeding is allowed by guides),

Pairs of gray angelfish are among the most common of the reef fishes found in the clear waters around the island.

Octopuses are frequently seen on night dives. They have an incredible ability to instantly change color and texture to blend with their surroundings.

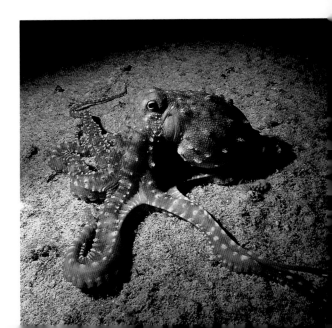

groupers will often assume positions over a section of the reef near where the feeding is being done and remain motionless.

As with a number of Cozumel reefs in this depth range, a good place to look for tight schools of margates, snapper and grunts is beneath overhangs, especially on the down current side of the reef sections. Also look for large angelfishes, and green and spotted morays.

12. YOCAB REEF

DEPTH: 35-60 FEET

(11-18 M)

CURRENT: MEDIUM TO

STRONG

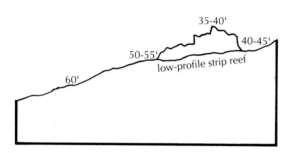

Yocab, also spelled Yucab, is a strip reef that is fairly close to shore, approximately 1¼ miles (2 km) south of Punta Tormentos (Point Tormentos), just north of Cardona Point. The reef itself is approximately 450 yards (409 m) long and sits on a sand bottom approximately 45 feet (14 m) deep on the shore side and 50 to 55 feet (15-17 m) deep on the offshore side. It is mostly a low-profile reef, rising an average of 8 to 12 feet (2-4 m) off the bottom making diving depths fairly shallow. The top of the reef averages 35 to 40 feet (11-12 m).

There is usually a medium to strong current moving south to north. Frequent sand channels run perpendicular through the reef, separating it into long sections. Large protected areas where fishes congregate can be found on the down current (north) end of these separate sections.

The resident fishes most often include small schools of silver margates, gray angelfish, French and blue-striped grunts, trunkfishes and porgies, as well as the usually illusive queen angelfish. Divers will also see several types of large black groupers cruising slowly against the current.

The reef ends abruptly as the bottom begins a gradual downward slope. If you continue on a straight line, you would eventually come to the top of the wall at Las Palmas. If you angle off to the left, you will run into the north end of Tormentos Reef. Dive guides will sometimes drop a group in this area and then dive one reef or the other depending on the direction of the current.

Photo tip. Photographers should investigate cuts and overhangs where they will find excellent opportunities to get closeup fish portraits. The fishes seem more intent on staying out of the current than in shying away from divers. As on most shallow reefs in Cozumel, pairs of large, white-spotted orange filefish and scrawled filefish are common. When taking pictures or shooting video of these fishes, keep in mind that they are "almost" always found in pairs. The male will usually try to draw you away from the smaller female. Watch where the female goes and place yourself between the two. The male will usually swim right by you to rejoin its mate.

This cluster of tube worms was found near the base of a coral head, facing into the current. These animals have sensors which will usually cause them to retract instantly because of changes in pressure waves, or light in the water.

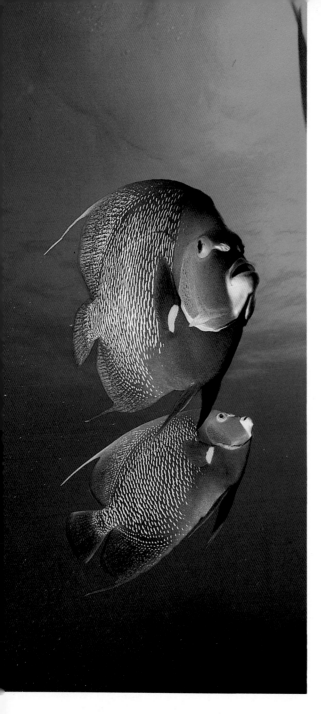

Pairs of large French angelfish will often approach divers along the drop-off at Punta Tunich. The current can become quite strong in this area, allowing divers to drift right up to fishes swimming against the current.

13. PUNTA TUNICH DROP-OFF

DEPTH: 50-130+ FEET

(15-39+ M)

CURRENT: MODERATE TO

STRONG

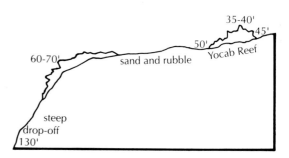

Punta Tunich or the Virgin Wall, is a wall dive located directly out from Punta Tunich and several hundred yards outside and parallel to Yocab Reef. The reef begins before the drop-off and continues over the edge. The top of the reef varies between 50 and 80 feet (15-24 m). Where the reef ends, there is little buildup of coral. The south end of the site is fairly barren with a steeply sloping drop-off. Divers will find lots of squirrelfishes tucked into crevices. Pairs of angelfishes are quite common and are often found heading directly into the face of the current. Aggressive pairs of gray and French angelfish will move amongst the approaching divers.

Vertical drop-off. The north end of this reef has by far the most interesting terrain. The wall becomes more of a vertical drop-off, and the reef is etched with depressions, cuts, tunnels and caves down to 130 feet (39 m). One of the reasons that this area has been designated the "Virgin Wall" is that you will see large sponges, deep water fans and even large branches of black coral.

An adult Spanish hogfish poses for a profile shot.

Large schools of grunts seem to flow over the reefs. They will often seek the shelter of the reef as divers approach.

The wall at Punta Tunich has several large green moray eels that are accustomed to being fed by a few of the local guides. The antics between these guides and eels offer unique photo and video opportunities. Guides will often hold and caress the eels.

Caution: unpredictable current. This site usually experiences strong currents which wisk you along. These currents are unpredictable, not only changing direction from north to south, but also into down currents.

14. SAN FRANCISCO REEF

DEPTH:	40-100+ FEET
	(12-30+ M)
CURRENT:	MODERATE TO
	STRONG

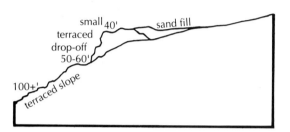

San Francisco Reef is a popular strip reef located approximately a kilometer offshore from San Francisco Beach. The reef sits at the edge of a small drop-off and runs roughly parallel to shore for about 450 yards (409 m). The maximum depths here are between 50 and 60 feet (15-18 m). In some places the top of the reef rises to within 40 feet of the surface.

The top of the reef is sand and rubble, with a sloping drop-off. Most of the coral is at, or over the edge of the lip. The reef is terraced, with a deep drop-off at the north end. Currents here can sometimes be very strong.

There is a good variety of reef fishes, including the ever present pairs of French and gray angels, queen angels, orange and spotted filefish, porgies, jacks, and lots of parrotfishes.

The effects of Hurricane Gilbert in 1988 can still be seen here. Sand has backed up against the inland side of the reef.

The few tunnels and cuts beneath the reef are quite extensive and definitely worth exploring. Lobsters in the 10- to 15-pound range are frequently seen in deep holes on the sandy bottom.

On the top of the wall, look for fields of tube worms. Hermit crabs are also very abundant. Rays are often seen feeding in the sandy area on the inside of the reef. On the lip of the drop-off, you will find numerous cleaning stations with tiny cleaner wrasse and juvenile hogfish removing parasites from surgeonfishes, small groupers, and a variety of other fishes.

Many ceilings of tunnels and caves are covered with brightly colored rope sponges.

Photo tip. Photographers will find that squirrelfishes are easier to photograph here than in most areas. Approach them slowly and they are less likely to dart into their nearby hole.

The wall outside of San Francisco Reef is referred to as San Francisco Wall. The drop-off is terraced between 60 and 100 feet (18-30 m). There is little coral structure buildup on these terraces, so only the inside reef is dived, and this site is always used as the second dive on a two-tank trip.

The resident gray angelfish often act accustomed to divers at San Francisco Reef.

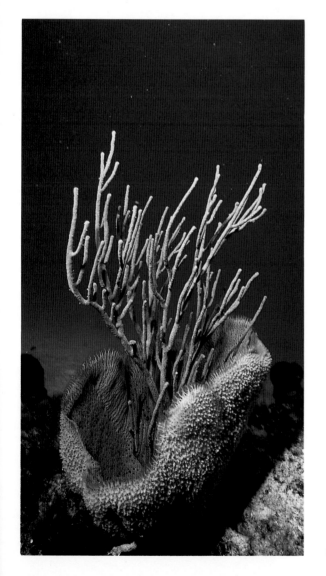

These corky sea fingers are growing from a vase sponge.

Large anemones are a frequent sight on the deep walls of Santa Rosa.

15. SANTA ROSA REEF

DEPTH:	30-130+ FEET
	(9-39+ M)
CURRENT:	MODERATE TO
	STRONG

Black groupers are common at Santa Rosa Reef. These are among the largest marine animals that divers usually encounter underwater.

This interesting area can be divided into three very distinct parts by the appearance of the reef, the configuration of the drop-off, and the predominance of certain varieties of fishes and invertebrates. Unless the current is really strong and you swim with it throughout the dive, it is impossible to see all of Santa Rosa Reef on one tank of air.

The current along the entire length of Santa Rosa is usually moderate to brisk and normally runs south to north. It is often enjoyable to swim a little ways out from the edge of the reef, and cruise slowly (sometimes fly) along watching the reef, and checking the blue water for something big to come by.

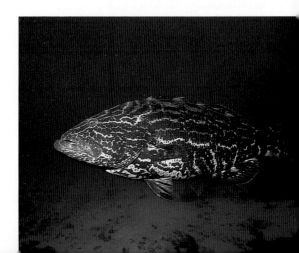

Caution: unpredictable current.
Occasionally, the current can be strong and
unpredictable. You can generally just drop
behind an overhang or into a cut or cave to get
out of the current. Once in a while, however,
there can be a down current which runs up
over the top of the reef and straight down the
wall. When this occurs, it is advisable to stay
on the shoreward side of the reef, which is
well-protected.

South Section

The southernmost part of Santa Rosa has a
steeply sloping solid wall that continues into
very deep water. As with the entire section of
reef, there is a flat sandy area on the shore side
where divers are always dropped to begin the
dive. This area is approximately 50 feet (15 m)
deep at the south end of the reef where the
sandy bottom abuts against the inside of the
reef. The reef formation itself is built up on the
lip of the drop-off. This section of reef is mostly
an unbroken ridge, which rises to about 45 feet
(14 m).

The majority of fishes you will see in this
area are large angels, a variety of squirrelfishes
and the usual assortment of small tropicals.
Looking out toward blue water, you will
usually see a large number of ocean triggerfish,
and an occasional small school of pelagics
such as African pompano, crevalle jacks,
horse-eye jacks, rainbow runners and bar
jacks. Solitary barracuda up to three feet (1 m)
in length are also fairly common. In past years
divers occasionally saw one or two blacktip or
lemon sharks along this wall at depths below
80 feet (24 m). However, shark sightings at
Santa Rosa are becoming rare because of the
increasing number of divers.

Middle Section

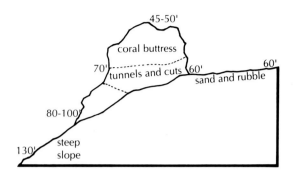

The sand bottom on the shore side of the reef
is about 60 feet (18 m) deep and the terrain
here begins to take on a much more interesting
appearance. The strip reef at the lip of the
drop-off is broken into sections. Although the
wall itself is still fairly steeply sloped and solid,
there are lots of swim throughs—tunnels and
cuts that are big enough to swim through
easily—caves and overhangs in the coral. Most
of these areas have sandy floors, but on the
ceilings of the tunnels, you will find an
interweaving of brightly colored rope sponges,
orange encrusting sponges, and brown tub and
barrel sponges. This site is in the 50- to 60-foot
(15-18 m) depth range.

Here, divers will encounter large black
grouper, barracuda, spotted morays and large
green morays. The eels in this area are
obviously used to being fed by the guides
because they will come out and greet divers,
or swim freely inside the tunnels during the
day. Spotted eels will also often be found
curled up on the sandy floors of some of the
tunnels, protruding from the coral walls, or
twisting their way around the surfaces of the
reef.

Cowfish and barracuda are commonly seen
inside or around the mouths of tunnels and
cuts at the top of the drop-off. Approach
barracuda slowly. If you see them change from
silver to dark with obvious vertical lines, it
usually indicates that they are getting agitated
or that they are hunting. Although barracuda
are generally not dangerous, don't corner them
and do not get too close when they display
such markings.

This is also a particularly good area to photograph or shoot video of queen angelfish, which will often be seen in groupings of as many as six fish of varying sizes.

There is a long area in this middle section where the reef structure is not built up at the lip of the drop-off. The top of the steeply sloping wall is approximately 60 feet (18 m) in this area.

North Section

Here, the top of the reef remains broken, but the drop-off becomes more vertical. You can swim through tunnels from the inshore side and end up looking straight down with nothing but dark blue below you. The top of the wall rises to between 30 and 40 feet (9-12 m) in this area. The flat sandy area on the inside of the reef is approximately 50 feet (15 m) deep.

The fish life on top of the reef at this end of Santa Rosa changes quite drastically. There are usually large schools of creole wrasse and many varieties of parrotfishes. There are lots of cleaning stations, as well as interesting invertebrates such as purple sponges, whip corals, sea rods and corky sea fingers.

There is a noticeable change in the reef structure as you get to the end of the northern section of Santa Rosa. A number of wide sandy channels cut between sections of the reef. The reef ridge turns into a patch reef, with the separate coral heads becoming progressively less massive. Watch for schools of fish in the top of the water column as you decompress at 15 feet (5 m). Schools of bar jacks, creole wrasse and baitfish are quite common.

16. PASO DEL CEDRAL REEF

DEPTH:	35-60 FEET
	(11-18 M)
CURRENT:	MODERATE TO
	STRONG

Paso Del Cedral is a patch and strip reef, about 250 yards (227 m) in length, which is frequently broken by perpendicular channels. It is located at the north end of Dalila (at Point Cedral) and to the east (or shore side) of the south end of Santa Rosa Reef. This wide reef sits on a relatively flat sand and rubble bottom in 55 to 60 feet (17-18 m) of water. The current, which fluctuates from moderate to strong, almost always runs in a south to north direction. The top of the reef varies between 35 and 50 feet (11-15 m), and gradually slopes upward at the north end.

A six-foot (2 m) green moray lives in a large coral head situated at the southern end and just on the shoreward side of the reef. However, the eel is used to being fed and will only pose for photographers who bring along squid, scraps of shell fish or other delicacies.

Schooling fishes. Paso Del Cedral is one of the best reefs to obtain good photographs of schooling fishes. Many different types of fish school here and the fishes are not too skittish. A large school of black and yellow porkfish crowd the caves and overhangs at the south end of the reef. These large fish make excellent subjects and will allow divers to join them out of the current. Inside the various sections of the reef, there is a maze of tunnels, caves and overhangs, where schools of grunts, snapper and margates can be found. Trunkfishes are

Large spider crabs are a common sight in tunnels and recesses.

A large school of porkfish are usually found under an expansive ledge and in the caves at Paso Del Cedral.

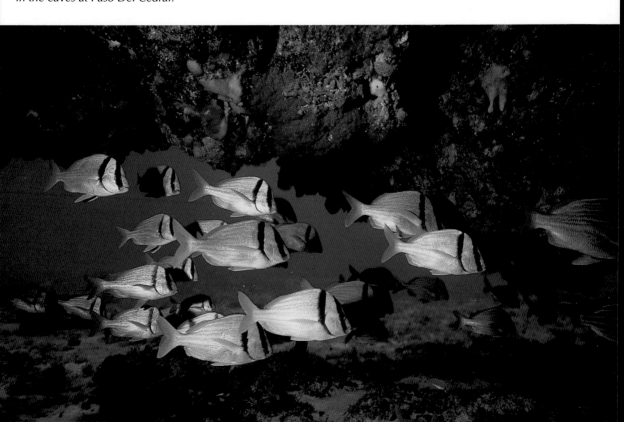

commonly seen in groups of two to six. It is also quite common to see varieties of parrotfishes, pairs of filefishes, large spider crabs, southern stingrays and solitary barracuda.

Although 60 feet (18 m) is the maximum depth on this dive, it is a good first dive for photographers because most of the best subjects are found close to the bottom. If done as a second dive, bottom time would be very limited.

There are many interesting animals that can be found in the sand flats. Here, a large southern stingray lies motionless, partially covered with sand.

17. LA FRANCESA REEF

DEPTH:	40-65+ FEET
	(12-20+ M)
CURRENT:	MODERATE

La Francesa Reef (The French Lady) is a long, wide reef on the shore side of the drop-off between the north end of Palancar Reef and the south end of Santa Rosa Reef. There is a flat sand bottom about 40 feet (12 m) deep on the shore side. The reef itelf is approximately 50 to 70 feet (15-21 m) wide in most places, and rises very little above the level of the sandy bottom on the shore side.

On the offshore side of the reef, there is a small wall that descends steeply to a gently sloping sand and rubble bottom approximately 60 to 65 feet (18-20 m) deep. From there the bottom terraces down to the lip of the drop-off. There are a few sand channels completely separating sections of the reef, but most of the reef is continuous and unbroken.

Lots of cuts, overhangs and caves can be found here. Small branches of black coral hang from the ceilings of caves and tunnels. Queen angelfish, cowfish and various types of filefishes are very common at this site. Usually, a few small schools of French grunts and blue-striped grunts are tucked under the overhangs.

18. DALILA REEF

DEPTH:	25-80 FEET
	(8-24 M)
CURRENT:	MODERATE TO
	STRONG

A colony of tube worms filters the water for drifting plankton.

Dalila is a strip reef with a small drop-off or mini-wall that continues in a northerly direction from the north end of Palancar Shallows. The reef is named after the nearby Dalila Ranch. Dalila is actually a series of strip reef sections, separated by wide sandy channels. The sand bottom averages between 45 and 65 feet (14-20 m), but drops to as deep as 80 feet (24 m) in some places. Therefore, it is important to watch your depth, especially if you are on the second dive of the day. At the south end there are many caves, overhangs and cuts. The reef gets shallower as you move to the north. In places, the top of the reef comes to within 25 feet (8 m) of the surface.

Dalila Reef offers a multitude of small invertebrates to photograph or videotape. This star-eyed hermit crab is a typical resident of the reef.

Large friendly grouper. The first thing one notices at Dalila is the presence of many large, friendly grouper. If a diver begins to feed the fish, aggressive chubs will charge in to grab the morsels. This usually causes the groupers to drift away from the action, but they never stray very far from the divers. In fact, they will often appear unexpectedly, cruising effortlessly across your path or turning, with seeming indifference, directly in front of you when you least expect it.

This reef is well known as a good place to explore for large, fat, green moray eels. They can usually be found tucked into and under low-lying ledges at the bottom of the coral heads. Some of these green eels measure up to seven feet (2.1 m) in length.

If the current is strong, and you don't spend much time poking around in the lee of the coral heads, you will come to the end of the reef in an area that is between the south ends of La Francesa and Paso del Cedral. Both of these reefs begin at a depth of about 35 feet (11 m). Here you will encounter whitespotted filefish and scrawled filefish. If you observe these fish over a period of time and try to get close to them, you will notice that they are usually found in pairs, as are gray angelfish and French angelfish. The larger fish is presumably the male. Most of the coral heads, especially the brain corals, are covered with unusually large Christmas tree tube worms.

This reef is a very good site for photography and video, although it is not chosen as a first dive site very often because of its proximity to Palancar and Columbia. It is a little too deep for a second dive. It requires a longer surface interval and you have to spend this interval

Orange tube sponges are a familiar sight on Cozumel's reefs.

without being able to use the time to motor back north toward your resort. Therefore, diving here as a second site puts you back at your resort much later in the day.

Palancar Reef

Palancar Reef is the reef that is most often identified with Cozumel. It is actually a conglomeration of a number of different sections of reef that extend over three miles along the southwestern edge of the island. These sections are about a mile offshore, and offer a variety of structures and configurations.

19. PALANCAR SHALLOWS

DEPTH: 15-70 FEET

(5-21 M)

CURRENT: USUALLY LIGHT

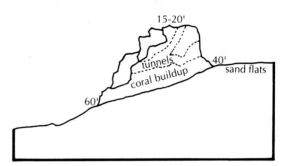

This site is also called Palancar Gardens and is located inside of and parallel to the entire length of the Palancar drop-off. At the northern end, Palancar Shallows is a strip reef, with a small drop-off on the offshore side of the reef. The inside of the reef is a flat sandy bottom in 40 feet (12 m) of water.

At the south end of Palancar Shallows, the reef structure rises only slightly above the sand bottom on its shore side. The reef then extends continuously to the Palancar Caves drop-off where the gently sloping sand and rubble bottom is between 60 and 70 feet (18-21 m) deep. As you swim father to the north, the sand bottom on the shore side of the reef gets gradually shallower until reaching depths of 20 to 25 feet (6-8 m). In places, the top of the reef structure rises to within 15 to 25 feet (5-8 m) of the surface.

This interesting reef is between 40 and 80 feet (12-24 m) in width in most places, and is full of caves, overhangs and cuts. The northern part of Palancar Shallows is located on the inside of the northern end of the Palancar Reef area. This long, narrow section of reef has extensive cuts and valleys, with lots of finger canyons and tunnels penetrating the formation. The ceilings of most caves and tunnels are crowded with bright orange rope sponges and various types of algae. There are many massive pinnacles on the outer edges of the reef. On the walls of the interior cuts, there are many medium-sized, deep-water gorgonians extending into these openings.

Divers will find only a few sea fans, but lots of whip corals and brain corals. Queen angelfish are plentiful, as are French and gray angels. Cleaning stations, mostly manned by juvenile hogfish, can be found everywhere around the reef. Cowfish, three-foot (1 m) barracuda, and schools of chubs and creole wrasse are common. The northern end of Palancar Shallows has greater numbers of tropical fishes.

20. PALANCAR HORSESHOE

DEPTH:	30-100+ FEET
	(9-30 M)
CURRENT:	MODERATE

The Horseshoe is one of the most popular places to begin a drift dive at Palancar. This area was named because of the large U-shaped cut in the reef structure. The top of the "U" is at the drop-off, with the bottom of the "U" cut into the reef and pointing toward shore. The top of the reef around the horseshoe is approximately 30 feet (9 m) deep, and falls to about 65 feet (20 m) at the outside edges of the base.

In 1985, a solid bronze, modernistic sculpture of Christ, measuring over 13 feet (4 m) in height, was placed here on a massive cubic base. When Hurricane Gilbert roared through the island in 1988, it knocked over the statue, which was then moved to Chancanab. The hurricane filled in much of the horseshoe with sand. Today, a lot of the sand has been swept away by the ever-present currents, and the base of the statue is exposed. Where once the bottom of the horseshoe was flat, it now has a sloping bottom.

This dive is usually done as a 60- to 80-foot (18-24 m) dive. As you follow the reef to the north of the horseshoe, you will find a labyrinth of caves, tunnels and passageways throughout the reef structure. There are still some large gorgonian fans, although there is not too much fish life except for schools of creole wrasse, chubs, angelfishes and yellowtail snapper. These fishes will follow groups of divers as they explore the spectacular terrain. Other schooling fishes that are occasionally seen here are ocean triggers and horse-eye jacks.

Spent air percolates up through the top of the reef forming a wall of bubbles rising along the route divers follow inside the reef. The outside wall drops vertically to a steep rubble slope, beginning at a depth of about 100 feet (30 m).

Large Nassau groupers are frequently seen in and around the horseshoe near the Palancar drop-off. These friendly groupers will often patiently pose for photographers.

The shallow reef that stretches along the west coast harbors a variety of corals including this whip coral.

A diver gets into a stare down with a balloonfish.

Schools of blue tangs will swim above the reef and then, as if on a prearranged signal, will stop in unison to feed for a few minutes in the same location.

21. PALANCAR CAVES

DEPTH: 20-100+ FEET
           (6-30 M)

CURRENT: LIGHT TO
           MODERATE

Palancar Caves is the area of Palancar Reef located south of the horseshoe. This site actually covers a distance of between two to three miles (1.2-1.9 km) of reef so it is impossible to see all of the Palancar Caves in only a few trips. In most places, the bottom on the shore side of the reef consists of flat, pure white sand with depths ranging from 30 to 40 feet (9-12 m). However, the reef structure occasionally extends into the shallows, joining with the southern part of Palancar Shallows. In some places, the sand bottom on the inside of the reef is only 20 feet (6 m) deep. However, the sand channel that separates Palancar Caves from Palancar Shallows dips to between 40 and 60 feet (12-18 m).

The broad reef structure of Palancar Caves is honeycombed with an extensive network of caves, tunnels, and pinnacles with intermittent sand falls and channels. The outside of the reef drops vertically to a steeply sloping sand and rubble drop-off, that begins at about 100 feet (30 m). Most dive operations set maximum depth limits at 90 feet (27 m). The dive guides will then escort divers slowly up to shallower depths between 30 and 40 feet (9-12 m) to finish the dive on top of the reef.

Schools of friendly and aggressive gray chubs and yellowtail snapper greet divers as they enter the water. Divers will find a few large deep water gorgonian fans protruding from the sides of the cuts in the coral. Small pinnacles, 30 or 40 feet (9-12 m) in height, are spaced at irregular intervals along the outside edge of the drop-off. There are also lots of encrusting sponges on the reef.

Although there are not many schooling fishes in this area, there are a large number of unusual fishes, including trunkfishes, cowfishes, puffers, spotted drums, filefishes and hamlets.

The currents generally run from the south to the north and are usually light to moderate in strength.

22. COLUMBIA GARDENS

DEPTH:	5-25 FEET
	(2-8 M)
CURRENT:	LIGHT TO
	MODERATE

The Palancar Caves area lends itself to photo opportunities because there are so many interesting animals clinging to drop-offs and pinnacles. Here, a diver floats above a wall adorned by a colorful vase sponge.

Columbia Gardens is a shallow reef that parallels the shoreline on the inside of the main reef. The relatively flat bottom which rarely dips below 25 feet (8 m) is sand and rubble. The reef is made up of a continuous string of large, high-profile coral heads, some of which come to within a few feet of the surface. Because of the shallow depth, this area makes an excellent second dive site to complement a wall dive at Maracaibo, Punta Sur or the Columbia Pinnacles.

This site is a beautiful area, teeming with marine life. Almost every type of tropical fish that is common to Cozumel can be found here. Keep an eye on the wide sandy area on either side of the reef where southern rays can often be seen feeding on shellfish. Even large loggerhead turtles have been spotted here.

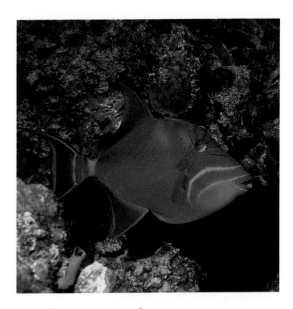

Columbia Gardens, although heavily damaged by hurricane Hugo, has a tremendous amount of photogenic marine life. This site seems to have an unusually large population of queen triggers.

23. COLUMBIA PINNACLES

DEPTH:	15-110+ FEET
	(5-33 M)
CURRENT:	MODERATE TO
	STRONG
LEVEL:	EXPERIENCED

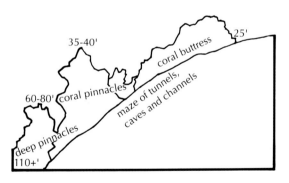

The Columbia Pinnacles is located between the south end of Palancar Reef and Punta Sur Reef. This Columbia Reef site has an impressive drop-off combined with spectacular massive pinnacles that rise from very deep water to within 60 to 110 feet (18-33 m) of the surface.

There is an extensive buildup of coral that begins in water 20 to 40 feet (6-12 m) deep. This coral buildup rises as it continues out toward the edge of the wall. The top of the formations come within 15 feet (5 m) of the surface in some places. The coral growth follows the contour of the slope into deeper water and become more extensive at the actual drop-off.

Steeply sloping sand channels wind in and around sections of the reef. The top of the main reef itself ranges in depth from 70 to 90 feet (21-27 m). Dive guides usually limit divers to a depth of 85 to 90 feet (26-27 m).

Often, divers encounter large grouper, turtles and eagle rays while winding over and around the spectacular formations. For the sheer majesty of the terrain, this area is unbeatable. In the blue expanse, divers will find large schools of yellowtailed snapper, horse-eye jacks, Bermuda chubs, creole wrasse, and a wide variety of other jacks. This is a great place to spot large fish.

At certain times of the year, eagle rays and schools of small blacktip sharks appear at Columbia and have been known to frequent the same area for weeks at a time.

Caution. Because of the depths and currents, this area is recommended for experienced divers.

Bright red, deep-water gorgonians are very common throughout the Punta Sur Reef area.

24. PUNTA SUR REEF

DEPTH:	80-130+ FEET
	(24-42 M)
CURRENT:	OFTEN STRONG
LEVEL:	EXPERIENCED

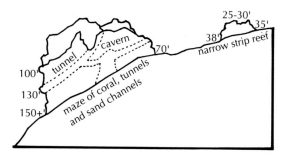

Punta Sur Reef is a deep wall dive located to the south of Columbia Reef just off Punta Sur (South Point). The top of the wall is

Punta Sur is quickly becoming one of the most popular dive destinations among Cozumel's southern reefs. A diver glides beneath an overhang at 110 feet (33 m), where colorful sponges and deep water gorgonians are plentiful.

Arrow crabs are found almost everywhere you look on the shallow reefs in Cozumel.

Blue chromis are very common on shallow to mid-depth reefs throughout the western coast of Cozumel.

A diver gets a close-up look at a large white margate under a ledge.

approximately 80 to 100 feet (24-30 m) deep. It is the farthest south of the reefs that have massive coral buildup at and over the lip of the drop-off. This area is honeycombed with incredible, massive caverns and tunnels carved into the wall mostly at depths between 80 and 140 feet.

Fabulous tunnel complex. Punta Sur offers the largest underwater rooms and chambers that can be found in Cozumel, and a fabulous complex of interconnecting tunnels and mysterious dead-end caves. Vertical columns and windows to the interior create spectacular lighting effects inside the reef. Some operations have begun to refer to part of this area as the

Balloonfish will ingest water to cause their bodies to expand and their spines to protrude at right angles from their bodies. This is done as a defense mechanism to discourage potential predators.

Cathedral. At one point, there is a tunnel which can be entered at 100 feet (30 m) and exited at 130 feet (39 m).

Fishes are not abundant at this site, although large angels and squirrelfishes are common. There is a fair chance that divers will see nurse sharks in the caves, and rays feeding in the sand or flying by along the drop-off. Most of the caverns and tunnels have sandy bottoms, so be sure to control buoyancy as you make your way through the tunnels and caverns. The ceilings of most caves, tunnels, and overhangs are covered with a jumble of orange and purple rope sponges.

This is an advanced boat dive. Dive profiles are set so that the maximum depth is a minimum of 110 feet (33 m). Before dive guides take groups to this area, they need to be assured of diver skill levels.

Inside the drop-off at Punta Sur, there is a shallow strip reef on a flat sandy bottom that lies in about 35 feet (11 m) of water. This area is usually referred to as Punta Sur Shallows.

25. MARACAIBO REEF

DEPTH: 60-130+ FEET
(18-39+ M)

CURRENT: OFTEN STRONG

LEVEL: EXPERIENCED

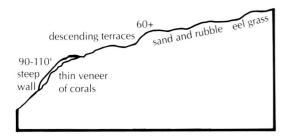

Maracaibo Reef is one of the two southernmost dive sites on the island. Maracaibo consists of reef terraces extending outward from the southeastern point of the island. There are three separate sections of reef located just offshore from Punta Celarain (Point Celarain), within sight of the Point Celarain Lighthouse. The tops of these reef terraces range from 60 to 120 feet (18-36 m), getting deeper as you get closer to the actual drop-off. The lip of the drop-off slopes gradually deeper as you move farther away from Point Celerain. When you go over the edge of the wall, the drop-off begins with a steep slope between 90 and 120 feet (27-36 m). A sheer vertical wall with some undercuts starts between 130 and 150 feet (39-45 m).

Caution. Maracaibo is strictly a boat dive which should be left to experienced divers who can deal with strong, variable currents and extreme depths. Because of the depth, no-decompression bottom time is limited to only a few minutes. All divers at Maracaibo should end the dive with a three to five minute safety stop at 15 feet (5 m). If divers go over the limits and require decompression stops, they will be forced to conduct them while drift diving in open ocean. For this reason, it is important for all divers in a group to stay together so that the boat captain can keep close track of the entire group. The next stop after the south point of Cozumel is a long way off.

Caution. Descend close to the edge of the drop-off, because currents can be strong and unpredictable. While currents usually run parallel to the reef, they frequently run away from the drop-off towards the shallows. Sometimes there is even a down current over the wall. If you drop to the bottom away from the lip, you may have to kick hard or pull yourself along the bottom to get to the drop-off, wasting precious air, time and energy.

On many reefs squirrelfishes can be found in almost every hole and crevice.

A diver cruises down over the lip of the drop-off at Maracaibo. Although the reef structure is not as extensive here as it is on Punta Sur, Palancar and Santa Rosa, the number of pelagics encountered in this area sometimes make this advanced dive very exciting.

The top of the reef is generally flat with sand, rubble, and scattered coral heads. There are a few areas with some interesting caves and tunnels along the wall. However, the wall itself in most areas within recommended sport diving depth limits is not very interesting.

Large pelagics. The real attraction offered here is the chance to encounter large pelagics. Because of the many divers who visit Cozumel, most large animals stay away from the more popular reefs. Eagle rays, sharks and schools of jacks are now only found in the more remote areas such as Maracaibo. Large groupers, weighing up to 200 pounds (91 kg) and measuring five feet (2 m) in length, and huge loggerhead sea turtles are also commonly seen at Maracaibo.

Maracaibo shallows. The higher terraces at Maracaibo are much shallower toward Point Celerain. The bottom along some of these terraces is in the 50- to 60-foot (15-18 m) range. In this area, you will find many large coral heads and a variety of deep water corals. Schools of grunts and snapper are usually present, and divers will frequently encounter nurse sharks crammed inside small crevices.

Feather duster tube worms are common residents of the eel grass beds found in the shallows.

White-spotted moray eels, which grow to between four and five feet in length, are a common sight and will often come all of the way out of the reef.

Large sponges are a common sight along the top of drop-offs.

Pelagic animals, such as this gray reef shark, are often encountered on advanced current dives at such locations as Barracuda Reef and San Juan Reef. Permission from the harbor master and advanced diving skills are required to visit these sights.

LESS FREQUENTED SITES

The sites listed below are either seldom visited by dive boats, or are for very experienced divers and require prior arrangements.

26. BARRACUDA REEF

27. SAN JUAN REEF

DEPTH:	70-80 FEET
	(21-24 M)
CURRENT:	VERY STRONG
LEVEL:	VERY EXPERIENCED

These reefs are located at the extreme northwestern end of the island. Dives at these reefs require making prior arrangements with the dive operator and must be cleared through the harbor master's office. Only a few operations visit these sites. Trips are limited to no more than six divers and all divers must be very experienced. The currents are usually very strong and unpredictable in this area.

Both areas offer fairly flat, strip reefs in the 70- to 80-foot (21-24 m) depth range. The main incentive for diving these areas is the chance to see large animals. Schools of jacks, rays, sharks, barracuda and other pelagics are very common. The terrain is more uneven at the San Juan site, where the reef ends in a large, natural bowl. Jacks often congregate here.

28. CARDONA REEF

DEPTH:	20-30 FEET
	(6-9 M)
CURRENT:	LIGHT

Cardona Reef is a shallow, low-profile strip reef to the south of Cardona Point. The reef is located just offshore where the bottom averages 25 to 30 feet (8-9 m). This area is usually used as a beach dive or for snorkeling. The reef ridge rises an average of 15 to 26 feet (5-8 m) above the bottom, and has many ledges and overhangs.

29. PALANCAR DEEP

DEPTH:	60-120+ FEET
	(18-36+ M)
CURRENT:	LIGHT TO
	STRONG

Palancar Deep is located at the south end of Palancar Reef. The top of the reef averages 60 feet (18 m). There is a steep vertical wall here with a massive coral structure and an extensive network of tunnels and caves.

30. CHUN CHACAB REEF

DEPTH:	10-120+ FEET
	(3-36+ M)
CURRENT:	STRONG

Chun Chacab Reef is a wall southwest of Punta Celarain, between Maracaibo Reef and Punta Sur Reef. There is a wide sand fall between Punta Sur Reef and Chun Chacab that slopes steeply to 120 feet (36 m), before ending in a vertical drop-off. The lip of the drop-off, which has little coral buildup, is at approximately 100 feet (30 m). This site is seldom visited by dive boats.

On the shore side of the drop-off is a vast, gently sloping, sand and rubble bottom that extends outward from the beach between Columbia Lagoon and Punta Celerain. The bottom is typically covered with grasses and occasional small coral heads and sponges. Conch shells are very common in this area. Dolphins are frequently seen cavorting in the shallows and feeding upon the plentiful shellfish found here.

Large solitary barracuda are often seen cruising over the reef at night, hunting for food.

CHAPTER **VII** MARINE LIFE

Cozumel has a wonderful assortment of colorful, interesting and unusual marine life awaiting the visiting diver.

Although there are only a few potentially harmful animals, and these are not normally aggressive, divers should still be cautious as to what they touch. Most of the animals mentioned in the following sections are abundant in Cozumel waters.

INTERESTING OR UNUSUAL FISHES

Angelfishes

Cozumel has three predominant species of angelfishes that are commonly found throughout the reefs which run along the west coast of the island. Although there are several other species of angelfishes, the **French angelfish**, the **gray angelfish** and the **queen angelfish** are the most commonly seen.

The **gray angelfish**, (*Pomacanthus arcuatus*), like the French angelfish is almost always found in pairs. Its color is uniformly gray to grayish-brown. It has a white mouth and the inner surface of the pectoral fin is yellow. This species is usually the least timid of the large angels and will often approach and sometimes swim slow circles around divers. Its maximum size is 18 to 20 inches (46-51 cm).

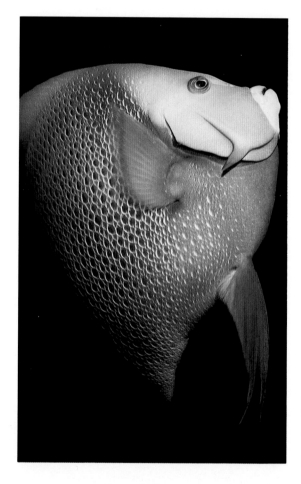

Gray angelfish (Pomacanthus arcuatus).

Swarms of silversides or baitfish are often seen flowing through the various chambers of the underground caves.

French angelfish (Pomacanthus paru).

The **French angelfish** (*Pomacanthus paru*) is predominantly black with its crescent shaped scales edged in bright yellow. It also has a white mouth and eyes that are ringed in bright yellow. The French angelfish is usually found in pairs and will occasionally approach divers. Its maximum size is 18 inches (46 cm).

The **queen angelfish** (*Holacanthus ciliaris*) is predominantly royal blue with yellow rims on the scales, and yellow pectoral, ventral and tail fins. Its face is usually yellow, with blue lips and a dark blue "crown" ringed in light blue on its forehead. Queen angelfish are generally shy and often are found in groups of three to six. Its average size is 8 to 14 inches (20-36 cm) with a maximum of 18 inches (46 cm).

Queen angelfish (Holacanthus ciliaris).

Balloonfish

The primary color of the **balloonfish** or **spiny puffer** (*Diodon holocanthus*) is usually tan to mottled brown, often with dark blotches. The pupil of the eye is an iridescent blue-green. This fish usually swims close to the reef or along rubble bottoms, blending in with the background. They will inflate with water when molested or threatened, resulting in a dramatic increase in size, and causing sharp spines that cover their body to project outward. Their average size is 8 to 14 inches (20-46 cm).

Balloonfish (Diodon holocanthus).

Honeycomb cowfish (Lactophrys polygonia).

Cowfishes

There are two species of cowfish found in Cozumel, the **honeycomb cowfish** (*Lactophrys polygonia*) and the **scrawled cowfish** (*Lactophrys quadricornis*). The primary color of the cowfish varies from blue to green. The honeycomb cowfish has a pattern that resembles a honeycomb. Both species have a sharp spine above each eye. Their maximum length is 18 inches (46 cm).

This fish is extremely shy and will avoid divers. They rely on camouflage to hide from predators.

Longsnout Sea Horse

The **longsnout sea horse** *(Hippocampus reidi)*, while still fairly rare, is now found more often on the shallow offshore reefs. Its color is variable, from yellow to brown or reddish-brown. While this species is very similar to the lined seahorse, it can be distinguished by the presence of tiny black spots on the head and body. This remarkable little animal anchors itself by wrapping its tail around sea rods, branches of gorgonians and sea grasses.

Longsnout sea horse (Hippocampus reidi).

Splendid toadfish (Sanopus splendidus).

Splendid Toadfish

The **splendid toadfish** (*Sanopus splendidus*) is one of two species of toadfish found in Cozumel. It is believed that the splendid toadfish, also called the "Cozumel catfish," is not found anywhere else in the Caribbean. This distinctive fish has a wide compressed head with whisker like appendages growing from its lower jaw. It has horizontal striping and some mottling, usually with charcoal gray or brownish gray lines over white. It has a bright yellow border on all of its primary fins. It grows to a length of 12 inches (31 cm).

The toadfish is commonly seen peering from the entrance of low crevices, perched on its pectoral or ventral fins. These crevices are most likely to be on sand and rubble bottoms along the sides of shallow and medium-deep strip reefs, or under coral heads closer to shore. At night when it is more active, you can often hear its low guttural mating call reverberating through the water.

Spotted Drum

The **spotted drum** (*Equetus punctatus*) is easily distinguishable as it has black and white bars on the head, and several stripes on the body. The rear dorsal and tail fin are black with white spots. Its maximum length is 10 inches (26 cm). This fish is unafraid of divers and can often be observed repeating circular or figure-eight swimming patterns. The juvenile has an extremely long dorsal fin.

Spotted drum (Equetus punctatus).

Trumpetfish (Aulostomus maculatus).

Trumpetfish

The **trumpetfish** (*Aulostomus maculatus*) has a long, thin body. Its usual color phase is brown to reddish-brown, but it can also be seen as silver or yellow. It can often be seen in a head down position, camouflaging themselves by mimmicking stalks of sea rods. Their average size is 18 to 30 inches (46-76 cm). Their maximum size is 3 feet (1 m).

Whitespotted Filefish

The **whitespotted filefish** (*Cantherhines macroceros*) has two distinct color phases. In one color phase, the body color is almost orangish or yellowish brown; in the other color phase the body is covered with white spots. This fish commonly ranges about the reef in what are believed to be mated pairs. Usually there is one of each color phase within the pair. They average 10 to 15 inches (26-38 cm) in size reaching a maximum of 18 inches (46 cm).

Whitespotted filefish (Cantherhines macroceros).

Interesting or Unusual Invertebrates

Christmas Tree Tube Worm

Feathered **Christmas tree tube worms** (*Spirobranchus giganteus*) are usually found on the surface of boulders or brain corals. They can appear in a myriad of colors including orange, red, maroon, blue, brown or yellow. They are worms whose tubes are embedded deeply inside the coral, so that only the expanded colorful branchiae are visible.

These worms sense changes in pressure and light, and will instantly retract into their tubes for protection. The spirobranchus has two diagonally projecting "Christmas trees," each with four to six whorls (or levels), which decrease in diameter as they get closer to the top.

Christmas tree tube worm (Spirobranchus giganteus).

Flamingo tongue cowrie (Cyphoma gibbosum).

Flamingo Tongue Cowrie

Flamingo tongue cowries (*Cyphoma gibbosum*) prey upon polyps of various corals, such as the purple sea fan. The cowrie inserts its proboscis into the cups and rasps away the living tissue with its rasp-like tongue called a radula. Unless molested or otherwise threatened, the flamingo tongue cowrie displays its orange and black mantle, which closely resembles the spots of a leopard. It is believed that this cowrie is so brazen about displaying its mantle because it is a major factor in ensuring reproduction. When the mantle is retracted, the outside of the shell has a pinkish-white to orangish-white tint.

Rock Mantis Shrimp

The common **rock mantis shrimp** (*Squilla empusu*) can be found in tiny recesses or caves in the limestone bottom in shallow offshore areas. Mantis shrimp have a razor-sharp finger, so divers should be careful about poking fingers down their dens. Their color varies from dark mottled green, to yellow-green or black. They can reach a maximum length of 4 inches (10 cm).

Rock mantis shrimp (Squilla empusa).

Hermit crab (Dardanus venosus).

Hermit Crab

Star-eyed **hermit crabs** (*Dardanus venosus*) can easily be recognized by the corneas of its eyes which are greenish-blue in color. They also have a dark central spot and radiating lines forming a star pattern. The maximum size of the carapace is slightly over 1 inch (2.6 mm) in diameter. Hermit crabs move their homes from shell to shell. As they outgrow the old one they look for a larger home that has been deserted.

Reef Squid

Reef squid (*Sepioteuthis sepioidea*) have fins that begin just behind the mouth and run the length of their body. These fins employ a rippling movement used to aid in propulsion. They swim with their short tentacles bunched, and are usually seen in groups of six to eight, moving slowly in shallow areas near shore. Their maximum length is about a foot (31 cm).

Reef squid (Sepioteuthis sepioidea).

Rough file clam (Lima scabra).

Rough File Clam

The **rough file clam** (*Lima scabra*) is a small, nondescript cream to brown colored shell. However, when the shell opens up, it displays a beautiful orange or red animal that extends long, streaming tentacles. The maximum length of the shell is approximately 3 inches (8 cm).

Bristle Worms

Two polychaete (many-bristled) worms, the **fire worm** (*Hermodice carunculata*) and the **red-tipped fire worm** (*Chloeia viridis*), are lined with thousands of glassy, needle-like bristles. At the slightest contact with the skin, the bristles penetrate and break off, causing inflammation, itching and numbness. The fire worm is particularly common on the reefs. They grow to about 10 inches (26 cm).

Fire worm (Hermodice carunculata).

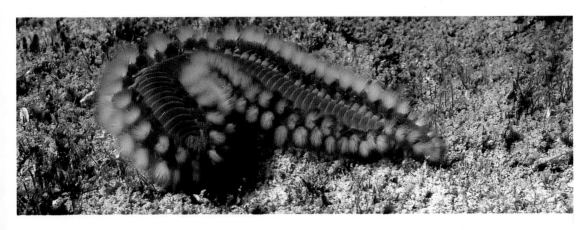

Fire Coral

The encrusting **fire coral** (*Millepora complanata*) is only one type of fire coral that exists on the reefs in Cozumel. It forms branching colonies. The coloration of most fire corals is usually a light brown or tan with white tips or edges. Upon close inspection, you can usually discern microscopic polyps which extend from pinhole-sized cups. Contact with any of the fire corals produces painful welts.

Eels

The **spotted moray** (*Gymnothorax moringa*) is the most common moray eel found in Cozumel. It has a white body with black spots or blotches all over its body. The spotted moray is also primarily a nocturnal feeder. It reaches a length of about 5 feet (1.5 m).

Morays are normally not a threat to divers. However, morays that are used to being fed by guides, will often come all the way out of the reef to search for morsels of food when divers approach. Morays have very bad eyesight and seek food using their sense of smell, which sometimes leads to fingers being mistakenly bitten. Divers should never stick their hands into holes in the reef. This may also lead to a nip by a defensive moray.

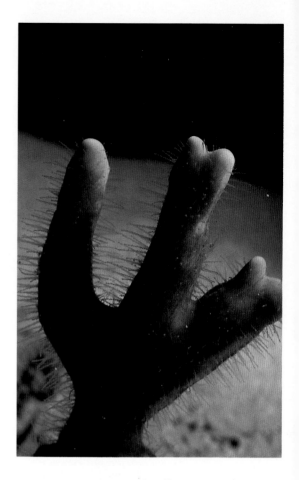

Fire coral (Millepora complanata).

Spotted moray (Gymnothorax moringa).

The **green moray** (*Gymnothorax funebris*) is the largest species of moray eel found in Cozumel. It has a uniform green or greenish-brown color. The moray is a nocturnal hunter. It receives a reputation for being viscious because it constantly opens and closes its mouth, not as a threat but simply to pass water over its gills. They can grow to a length of 7 feet (2.1 m).

Spiny Sea Urchins

The long-spined **black sea urchin** (*Diadema antillarum*) is normally nocturnal. During the day, they hide in reef crevices or aggregate in groups on the shallow bottom. At night these animals scatter over the sea floor, feeding on algae and turtle grass. Full grown adults are usually black. In younger specimens the color may be banded brown and black, or white and brown. The long spines of these animals contain toxins and can cause excruciating pain if the tips of the spines penetrate and break off under the skin.

Long-spined black sea urchin
(Diadema antillarum).

Green moray (Gymnothorax funebris).

Spotted scorpionfish (Scorpaena plumieri).

Spotted Scorpionfish

The **spotted scorpionfish** (*Scorpaena plumieri*) is a master of disguise. It is actually quite common, but rarely seen because it blends in well with a sand and rubble bottom and will not move unless molested. Its color is usually gray to light brown. The only time the fish is easy to spot is when it swims, exposing the top of its pectoral fins, that are banded in reddish brown, orange, black and yellow. Some specimens may grow to 18 inches (46 cm) in length. They are frequently found in pairs. These bottom dwelling rockfish have the ability to inject poison through the spines in their dorsal, anal and pelvic fins.

Yellow Stingray

The **yellow stingray** (*Urolophus jamaicensis*) has a smallish, yellow-brown body covered with blotches and spots. It has a tail with a venomous spine, that can inflict a painful sting. This ray is usually found on sand and rubble bottoms. Divers should avoid trying to grab or otherwise molest this animal which reaches a length of about 15 inches (38 cm).

Yellow stingray (Urolophus jamaicensis).

Appendix 1

Recompression Chamber

Sub-Aquatic Safety Services	**22387**
	VHF Channel 6

Dr. Pascual Piccolo
Calle 5 Sur 21-B, south of the Plaza
1/2 block east of Av. Rafael Melgar
Next to Discover Cozumel Diving

Cozumel has an excellent, privately owned, two-person hyperbaric chamber operated by an experienced staff. Divers may buy chamber insurance at most dive resorts for US$1.00 per diver per day of diving. I recommend that divers pay this nominal fee to help support the chamber even if one has additional insurance. If you do not have an emergency, but are interested in visiting the chamber facilities their office hours are from 8 A.M. to 8 P.M.

Hospital	**20140**
Ambulance	**20639**
Police	**20092**

Doctors

Listed below is a selection of English speaking doctors. Your hotel will be glad to recommend additional doctors or dentists.

M.F. Lewis, M.D.   **21616/20912**
50 bis #840, Bet. 11th & 13th Street
American
General practice

Carlos Peniche, M.D.   **21419/22919**
20 Av. Norte #425
24-hour service
Gynecology, fractures, pediatrics, trauma, intestinal disorders, hospitalization

Ricardo Segovia G. D.   **20741**
11 Av. Sur #101, Suite 2A
24-hour service
Gynecology, fractures, pediatrics, trauma, intestinal disorders, hospitalization

Paulino Calderon M.D.   **21440**
#181 Coldwell Av. at 30 Av.
24-hour service
General practice

Divers Alert Network (DAN)

The Divers Alert Network (DAN) operates a 24-hour emergency number **(919) 684-8111** (collect calls accepted if necessary) to provide divers and physicians with medical advice on treating diving injuries. DAN also maintains up-to-date information on the locations of recompression chambers accepting sport divers. In addition, they can organize air evacuation to the nearest recompression chamber.

Since many emergency room physicians do not know how to properly treat diving injuries, it is highly recommended that in the event of an accident, you have the physician consult a DAN doctor specializing in diving medicine.

DAN is a publicly supported, not-for-profit membership organization. Membership is $25 a year and includes a first aid manual, the dive safety magazine, *Alert Diver*, and emergency assistance service from Assist America, the most experienced assistance company in America. Assist America provides all DAN members with guaranteed emergency evacuation from anywhere for a medically necessary reason. Assist America provides multi-lingual, medically trained operators 24 hours a day at many locations throughout the world. DAN members are also able to buy either a $15,000 medical insurance policy for $20 a year or a $30,000 one for $25. The policy covers hospitalization, air ambulance and recompression chamber treatment for diving injuries. Divers should check with their insurance companies since many policies do not cover specialized treatment for diving accidents.

DAN's address is Divers Alert Network, Box 3823, Duke University Medical Center, Durham, NC 27710. Their non-emergency number is (919) 684-2948.

APPENDIX 2

USEFUL NUMBERS FOR VISITORS

Airlines

AeroCaribe	Cozumel 20928/20877
	Cancun 41231/42000
AeroCozumel	Cozumel 20928/20877
	Cancun 41231/42000
Continental	Cozumel 20487/20576
Mexicana	Cozumel 20263/20157/20133

Airport Immigration   20516

Ferry   20861

Long Distance Operator

2 Av. 5 Calle Norte, near Calle 1 Sur.
(On the Plaza)
You can call direct or collect from most resort hotels. By calling collect you can save the 70 percent tax.

Port Captain   20169

Post Office   20106

Avenida Rafael Melgar at Calle 7 Sur
(4 blocks south of the Plaza)
Hours: M-F 9 A.M. to 1 P.M., 3 to 6 P.M.;
Saturday 9 A.M. to 1 P.M.

Pharmacies

Farmacia Dori   20559
Adolfa Rosada Salas #20A

Los Portales   20741
Calle 11 Sur #11

Farmacia Joaquin   20125
East side of the Plaza

Photo and Video Services

Cozumel Images   23755/21665
Casa Del Mar Hotel
(under Sol Cribe bridge)
Most complete selection of photo and video rentals in Cozumel, film developing, photography and videography courses, professionally produced underwater video of your trip

Cozumel Underwater Video Service
#50 Calle 8 Norte
(4 blocks north of the Plaza & 1/2 block east of the water)
Video system rentals, prerecorded tapes, professionally produced underwater video of your trip

Dive Paradise   21007
601 Rafaelo Melgar
(South of the Plaza across from Navy Base)
35 mm camera rentals, professionally produced underwater video of your trip

Photo Safari   23581
Calle 5 Sur
1/2 block from the ocean)
Video & camera rentals, prerecorded tapes, professionally produced underwater video of your trip

One Hour Photo
Villa Mar Plaza
(Next to Banpais)
Slides, prints, cassettes, batteries

Tony Tate's U/W Video   21850/21444
8th Street
(Between water & 5th Av.)
Video system rentals, prerecorded tapes, professionally produced underwater video of your trip

APPENDIX 3

DIVE OPERATIONS

To telephone Cozumel from the United States add **011-52-987** before the five-digit local number.

North of San Miguel

Club Cozumel Caribe Divers
At the Club Cozumel Caribe
Tel: 20100

Downtown San Miguel

Adventuras Tropicales
On the Malecon north of the Plaza
Tel: 20393

Aqua Safari
Four blocks south of the Plaza
#39 Av. Melgar (the Malecon) at 7 Calle Sur
Tel: 20101/20661
Second location at Plaza Las Glorias
Tel: 20101/20661

Blue Bubble Divers
Blue Bubble Scuba School
Calle 3 Sur and 5a Av
Across from Hotel Aguilar
Two blocks south of the Plaza, 1 block from
the water
Tel: 21865

Bonanza Boat Trips
North of the Plaza on 2 Calle Norte
Tel: 20563

Caribbean Divers
#38 B Avenida Rafael Melgar
Three blocks south of the Plaza
Tel: 21080/21426

Cozumel Divers
(also Scuba Shack)
#221 Avenida Melgar
South of Calle Rosado Salas
Tel: 21076
(Also at Diver's Inn)

Deportes Acuaticos
Plaza Las Garzas
Four blocks north of the Plaza
Ave. Rafael E. Melgar and Calle 8
Tel: 20640

Discover Cozumel Diving
South of the Plaza
1/2 block east of Av. Rafael Melgar
#22 Calle Sur 5
Next to the Recompression Chamber
Tel: 20280
(Second location at Chancanab Lagoon)

Dive House
South side of Plaza
Between Av. Melgar and Av. 5
Tel: 21953

Dive Paradise
1. 601 Rafael Melgar
   (Main store)
   South of Plaza across from Navy Base
   Tel: 21007
2. #4 Calle 3 Sur
   Behind ORBI Dept.

Equalizers Scuba Center
A.R. Salas #72
Around corner from Pepe's Grill
Tel: 23611

Michelle's Dive Shop
5a. Ave. Sur in San Miguel
1/2 block south of Calle 1 Sur
Tel: 20947/20280

Ocean World
Calle 3 Sur and 5a. Av.
Tel: 20224

Palancar Divers
Palancar Diving Company
Avenida Juarez #17
11/2 blocks east of ferry pier
Tel: 21601

Pro Dive
Adolfo Rosado Salas Street and 5th Ave.
Tel: 20221

Seasports Scuba Center
Av. Rosado Salas S/N
Tel: 20380

Snorkozumel
#11A Calle 5 Sur
Three blocks south of Plaza
Between Av. Melgar and 5 Av.

Yocab Reef Divers
57 Av. Rosada Salas
Tel: 21842

South of San Miguel

Argonautas del Caribe
Las Velas Comples Costera Sur Km 2.85
Tel: 21232

Barracuda Hotel
No. 628 Prolongacion Sur
Ave. Rafael E. Melgar
Tel: 20002

Blue Angel Scuba School
Across from VillaBlanca Hotel
11/2 miles south of Plaza
Tel: 20913/21631

Casa Del Mar
(See Del Mar Aquatics)

Clear Water Divers
Calle 5 Sur
Tel: 20983

Del Mar Aquatics
(Main office)
Tel: 21833

1. Casa Del Mar
   Across from Casa Del Mar Hotel
   Tel: 21922

2. La Ceiba Beach Hotel
   At La Ceiba Hotel
   Tel: 21833/20379

Discover Cozumel Diving
At Chancanab Lagoon

Fantasia Divers
South of town at Sol Caribe Hotel
Tel: 20725

La Perla Hotel Diving
Tel: 20188

Playa Corona Diving
Playa Corona Beach Club
Calle 3 Sur
Tel: 21451

Scuba Cozumel Dive Shop
Across from Galapago Inn
Tel: 20627

Galapago Inn Dive Resort
One mile south of PLaza
Across from Galapago Inn
Tel: 20663/21133

Scuba Shack
Across from Scuba Inn and Ernesto's Fajitas
Tel: 20145

Viajes y Deportes Del Caribe
At Stouffer El Presidente
Tel: 20322

Appendix 4

Helpful Words and Phrases

General

I don't speak Spanish.	*No hablo Espanol.*
	(no ahb-low es-pan-yole)
I don't understand.	*No entiendo.*
	(no ent-e-yen-do)
How are you?	*Como esta usted?*
	(caw-mo es-tah oo-sted)
Very well, thank you.	*Muy bien, gracias.*
	(moo-ee be-yen, grahs-yas)
Come here, please.	*Venga aqui, por favor.*
	(veng-gah ah-key, poor fayvor)
What is your name?	*Como te llama?*
	(caw-mo tay yah-ma)
My name is...	*Me llamo...*
	(may yah-mo)
The bill please.	*La cuenta, por favor.*
	(lah kwen-tah por-fay-vor)
How much is it?	*Cuanto cuesta?*
	(kwen-toe kwess-tah)
One more	*Uno mas*
	(oo-no moss)
Hello/good day.	*Buenos dias.*
	(bway-nohss dee-ahss)
Thank you.	*Gracias.*
	(grah-see-ahs)
You're welcome.	*De nada.*
	(day nah-dah)
Goodbye.	*Adios.*
	(ah-day-ohss)
Yes.	*Si.*
	(see)
No.	*No.*
	(no)
Excuse me.	*Perdoneme.*
	(pair-dough-neh-may)
Where is...?	*Donde esta...?*
	(Doan-day ess-tah)
...a hotel?	*...un hotel?*
	(oon oh-tell)
...the toilet?	*...el bano?*
	(ell bahn-yoh)
...a good doctor?	*...un buen medico?*
	(oon bwayn may-dee-co)
When?	*Cuando?*
	(kwahn-do)
What?	*Que?*
	(kay)
Tomorrow	*Mañana*
	(mahn-yawn-ah)

Good	*Bueno*
	(bway-no)
Do you speak English?	*Habla usted Ingles?*
	(ab-la oo-sted ing-glace)
Two persons	*Dos personas*
	(dose pair-so-nahs)

Directions

Avenue	*Avenida*
Left	*Izquierda*
	(ees-ky-erh-day)
Right	*Derecha*
	(day-ray-chah)
North	*Norte*
South	*Sur*
Point	*Punta*
Street	*Calle*

Menu Terms

Beer	*Cerveza*
	(sir-vay-sah)
Bread	*Pan*
Cake	*Torta*
Coffee w/ cream	*Cafe con crema*
Coffee, black	*Cafe negro*
Chicken	*Pollo*
	(poi-yoh)
Eggs	*Huevos*
	(way-vohs)
Fried	*Frito*
Juice	*Jugo*
Ice	*Hielo*
	(he-ay-low)
Ice cream	*Helado*
Lobster	*Langosta*
Meat	*Carne*
Milk	*Leche*
	(letch-ay)
Roasted	*Asado*
Shrimp	*Camarones*
Soft drink	*Refresco*
Sugar	*Azucar*
Soup	*Sopa*
	(soap-ah)
Water	*Agua*
	(ag-wah)

INDEX

A **bold** faced page number denotes a picture caption.
An <u>underlined</u> page number indicates detailed treatment.